Overcoming Unintentional Racism in Counseling and Therapy

A Practitioner's Guide to
Intentional Intervention

Charles R. Ridley

Multicultural Aspects of Counseling Series 5

SAGE Publications
International Educational and Professional Publisher
Thousand Oaks   London   New Delhi

For information address:

SAGE Publications, Inc.
2455 Teller Road
Thousand Oaks, California 91320
E-mail: order@sagepub.com

SAGE Publications Ltd.
6 Bonhill Street
London EC2A 4PU
United Kingdom

SAGE Publications India Pvt. Ltd.
M-32 Market
Greater Kailash I
New Delhi 110 048 India

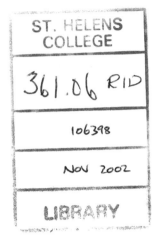

Printed in the United States of America

Library of Congress Cataloging-in-Publication Data

Ridley, Charles R.
  Overcoming unintentional racism in counseling and therapy: A practitioner's guide to intentional intervention / author, Charles R. Ridley
      p.   cm. — (Multicultural aspects of counseling series : vol. 5)
  Includes bibliographical references and index.
  ISBN 0-8039-4869-7. — ISBN 0-8039-4870-0 (pbk.)
  1. Counseling. 2. Racism. 3. Ethnocentrism. I. Title. II. Series.
  BF637.C6R53   1995
  361.3'23'08693—dc20   94-36551

                00   01   10   9   8   7   6

Sage Production Editor: Diana E. Axelsen

Contents

To Iris Rochell Ridley, my life's treasure

Acknowledgments

Many individuals contributed in various ways to the writing of this book. I am indebted to each of them. Thomas and Annabell Ridley, my parents, taught me spiritual values and the self-discipline needed to complete this type of undertaking. Faith Phippes, my cousin, awakened in me a passion for writing. Dr. Paul Pedersen had the wisdom to suggest I write a book on this topic. Dr. John Taborn was my intellectual mentor. He laid the foundation for my understanding of racism. Dr. Joseph Ponterotto provided an evenhanded critique and helped to shepherd the writing process.

The staff at Sage Publications deserves a special thanks. Marquita Flemming, aided by Dale Grenfell and Diana Axelsen, provided invaluable support. They believed in this project and made business a pleasure.

Several individuals at Indiana University should be acknowledged. Benita Banning typed numerous drafts of the manuscript. Her work was nothing short of excellent. Danielle Lingle and Bettina Kanitz, my doctoral students, have been an integral part of my multicultural research team. Many of my ideas emerged out of this think tank.

I am especially grateful to the team of reviewers: Professors Gerald Corey, Michael D'Andrea, Halford H. Fairchild, Allen E. Ivey, Tina Q. Richardson, and Jerome Taylor. Their comments were constructively critical and insightful, and helped sharpen the presentation. More importantly, their enthusiastic endorsement was pretty amazing.

Last but not least, Iris, Charles, and Charliss Ridley—my wife and children—were incredible sojourners during this lengthy pilgrimage. I am most blessed for having them in my life.

Preface

Two major traditions in the social sciences have been used to explain human behavior: an emphasis on the causes and an emphasis on the effects. Psychological theories are prominent in focusing on the causes of human behavior. Many of these theories are based on a common principle—that behavior is motivated by conscious or unconscious mental processes. These theories assert that when people discover the motivational sources of their behavior, they can better understand themselves and make constructive changes in their personalities. Classical psychoanalysis, with its emphasis on unconscious mental processes and early childhood experiences, elegantly represents this class of theories.

Theories that emphasize the causes of behavior are typically used to explain racism and other forms of oppression. They focus almost exclusively on the biases, prejudices, and bigotry of the racist. Thus proposals for change generally work from the inside out. These proposals encourage people to first explore their hidden bigotry. Once motives are unmasked and people begin to accept their bigotry, it is assumed that they will change and treat people of other races in a fair and equitable manner.

This book sets forth a different approach, examining counselor racism in light of its effects. Racism has many faces. Some of these faces are intentional, and others are unintentional. Whatever the face, racism is always harmful. Counselors with laudable intentions are often the ones most responsible for insidious acts of racism. This book pinpoints specific behaviors of counselors and describes how these behaviors adversely affect minority clients. Thus readers are challenged to examine the relationship between their behavior as counselors and the consequences of their behavior. For most counselors, this approach requires a paradigm shift from causal to consequential explanations of racism.

This approach does not minimize the relevance of personal motivation. Certainly counselors must come to terms with the causes of their behavior. When they see their bigotry, they should try to resolve it. But becoming self-aware and changing on the inside are only partial solutions to overcoming racism. Counselors must also identify specific racist behaviors, recognize the harmful consequences of their racism, and then deliberately change these behaviors. These steps should help counselors to beneficially serve minority clients. Unfortunately, this part of the solution is usually overlooked. In reading this book, many well-meaning counselors should discover that, despite their best intentions, they are unintentional racists.

Overcoming Unintentional Racism in Counseling and Therapy: A Practitioner's Guide to Intentional Intervention is for all helping professionals, including counselors, psychologists, social workers, psychiatrists, marriage and family therapists, student personnel professionals, nurses, and ministers. The book is analytical in its treatment of the topic, but it goes beyond problem analysis. This book offers solutions—concrete strategies to overcome unintentional racism in counseling and therapy. To accomplish these goals, the book is organized into two major parts. Part I, "Examining the Counselor's Unintentional Racism," contains six chapters. These chapters cover the nature, scope, history, and dynamics of racism in mental health service delivery. Particular attention is given to counselor unawareness of the problem. Part II, "Overcoming the Counselor's Unintentional Racism," consists of five chapters, each of which provides a specific strategy with a variety of practical recommendations.

I hope that readers will benefit by learning to become more effective service providers. More importantly, I hope that ethnic minority consumers will benefit by becoming recepients of responsive service delivery.

Charles R. Ridley
Bloomington, Indiana

PART I

Examining the
Counselor's Unintentional Racism

1

Minority Clients as Victims

Picture yourself as the victim of a driver running the red light. As a safety-conscious pedestrian, you walk to the corner and wait until the light turns green. Before entering the intersection, you look both ways, and then you proceed. When you get halfway across the street, however, tragedy strikes. The speeding car knocks you off your feet, leaving you badly bruised and disheveled, with a few broken bones.

Numerous explanations could account for the behavior of the driver. A young man, rushing his pregnant wife to the hospital, was distracted by her labor pains. The driver was intoxicated. The driver was negligent about auto maintenance, and the brakes on the car finally gave out. A pretty young lady walking down the street caught the driver's attention, resulting in his careless driving manner. The driver was temporarily blinded by the glare of the sun. The driver was a suspected burglar being pursued in a high-speed police chase.

Add an interesting twist to the story. This is not your first accident crossing the street. On many occasions, you and members of your family have encountered a car running out of control. Incidentally, tragedy never strikes your neighbor, Mr. Jones, even though he regularly walks the same streets as you and members of your family.

Understanding the Victim[1]

The preceding story, which is obviously fictitious, can nevertheless provide useful insights applicable to counseling. These insights should help the reader better understand what it means to be a victim and the importance of counselors being sensitive to the victim's plight. The story also sets the stage for the topic of this book—overcoming unintentional racism in counseling and therapy. Here are five thoughts to ponder.

1. Anyone Can Be a Victim

Few people go through life untouched by victimization. Victims of crime, of physical or sexual abuse, of mental cruelty, of natural disaster, of war, of a jealous lover, of deception and manipulation, of oppression, of their own careless actions—these and a host of other groups bear the marks of their trauma and injury.

Every victim has a unique story. The pedestrian crossing the street did not suspect impending danger. Although anyone in the wrong place at the wrong time can get hit by a car, no two victims have identical experiences. One of the great human tragedies is that some people are victimized many times over. The reality of being a victim is experienced by many people, and we should not close our eyes to the fact that anyone can be a victim.

2. The Victim May Not Be at Fault

Victims most often are the targets of forces outside of their control. The victimizer is typically another person. Ironically, people are sometimes victims of their own abuse, for example, those who set themselves up for failure, choose self-defeating lifestyles, or attempt suicide. Most of these self-abusive people are merely acting out their unresolved pain at having been someone else's victim in the past.

Because many victims are not responsible for their victimization, they should not be blamed. The pedestrian in the opening story made an honest but unsuccessful attempt to avoid an automobile accident. In our society, some victims experience double jeopardy. First, they are victimized. Then they are blamed for being a victim. This fundamental denial of responsibility further cripples the victim, who often internalizes irresponsibility and self-blame. However, victims do not deserve to be blamed anymore than they deserve to be victimized.

3. Intentions Are Not an Accurate Gauge for Measuring Victimization

People are victimized for many reasons. Sometimes victimization results from malicious intent: a clear and unequivocal decision on someone's part to harm. Sometimes victimization is unintentional: an outcome that is not the result of malicious intent. Many attempts to prove victimization are really attempts to prove malicious intent. Victimization, however, may reflect something beyond intentionality. It always involves action—the horrendous behavior of one person toward another. To the injured pedestrian, it does not matter whether the driver of the car was a criminal, a drunkard or a girl watcher. What really counts is the harm caused by the driver's actions.

4. Victims Need to Be Understood From Their Point of View

It is easy to think that you understand a victim when you really do not. The emotional toll on the victim is often discounted. Feelings of shame, self-blame, humiliation, rage, a sense of intrusion, violation, and vulnerability, or even the desire for revenge are common. These feelings may linger on long after the actual victimization. Many victims, because their feelings are unresolved, continue to play the victim role. As McCann, Sakheim, and Abrahamson (1988) explain, the scars of victims are often invisible, yet they leave profound persisting effects. To intervene in a meaningful way, counselors must realize the tremendous pain involved in being a victim and the tendency of many victims to avoid their pain. Counselors should also understand that every victim views his or her experience from a unique vantage point.

Understanding the victim is a challenge, especially for people who do not have this experience. The tragedy of not being understood as a victim is second only to the tragedy of actually being one. The empathy needed to really understand requires active listening, patience, and the willingness to set aside one's preconcieved ideas. Counselors who do not exhibit these qualities are likely to misunderstand the unique experience and perspective of the victim. Tragically, they may victimize their clients further through their lack of understanding.

5. When Victimization Is Selective and Repeated, It Is Not Just Victimization

When people victimize each other, it is appalling and a blight on society. The only positive aspect of victimization is its prevention. However, it remains a social enigma. For some people, it means they are repeatedly victimized.

Repeatedly being a victim, while others of similar status are not, indicates a larger problem. In the opening story, it could be argued that Mr. Jones is luckier, smarter, or better than the injured pedestrian. But this explanation does not seem plausible. A more realistic explanation is that there is a force working against the pedestrian, but not Mr. Jones. In that sense, the pedestrian is a selected victim.

Racism in Counseling and Therapy

Minority clients are selected victims. They are victims of racism in the mental health delivery system. This type of victimization is an almost unbelievable irony. Minority clients experience abuse, neglect, and mistreatment at the hands of counselors. The irony is that counseling is supposed to be helpful, and all clients deserve equitable treatment, regardless of their backgrounds. Counseling should be the most unlikely profession to victimize.

Unfortunately, racism in mental health delivery systems is not new, nor has it been adequately dealt with in the decades since the civil rights movement of the 1950s and 1960s. The history of racism in mental health care dates back to the early years of this country.

Thomas and Sillen (1972) reported on the history of racism in psychiatry. They focused primarily on the experiences of Black patients, but their observations are characteristic of the mistreatment of racial minority patients in general. Two quotes from their book capture this despicable legacy:

> Thus a well-known physician of the ante-bellum South, Dr. Samuel Cartwright of Louisiana, had a psychiatric explanation for runaway slaves. He diagnosed their malady as *drapetomania,* literally the flight-from-home madness, "as much a disease of the mind as any other species of mental alienation." Another ailment peculiar to black people was *dysaesthesia Aethiopica,* sometimes called rascality by overseers, but actually due to "insensibility of nerves" and "hebetude of mind." (p. 2)

> Actually, most asylums in the North excluded blacks—for example, the Indiana Hospital for the Insane did not take Negroes on the ground that they were not legal citizens of the state. . . . In the few asylums that sometimes admitted Negroes the ratio was one to several thousand white patients. Dr. John S. Butler, superintendent of the Hartford Retreat, attributed the

small number of blacks in his institution to their constitutional cheerfulness, which made them less vulnerable to insanity. The Northern psychiatrists "did not seem to see the contradiction in ascribing the lack of Negroes in their hospitals to their alleged general immunity to the disease and at the same time admitting that hospitals did not ordinarily admit Negroes." (p. 18)

Studies from the mid-20th century onward have documented the enduring pattern of racism in mental health care delivery systems. The literature has examined the effects of racism on members of various racial minority groups, including African Americans, Asian Americans, Hispanic Americans, and Native Americans. The literature has also reported on racism in a variety of treatment settings, including inpatient and outpatient settings. Table 1.1 lists authors of representative publications that report on racism in counseling and mental health care delivery. Several of these studies date back to the 1950s.

Despite these studies, however, the President's Commission on Mental Health (1978) documented the continuing problems encountered by minority clients:

Racial and ethnic minorities . . . continue to be underserved. . . . It makes little sense to speak about American society as pluralistic and culturally diverse, or to urge the development of mental health services that respect and respond to that diversity, unless we focus attention on the special status of the groups which account for the diversity. . . . Too often, services which are available are not in accord with their cultural and linguistic traditions. . . . A frequent and vigorous complaint of minority people who need care is that they often feel abused, intimidated, and harassed by non-minority personnel. (pp. 4-6)

Five years later, Jackson (1983), who has written extensively on race and psychotherapy, poignantly describes racism in counseling. Two of her comments highlight the problem:

In the psychotherapy relationship, characterized by close interpersonal interaction, aspects of racism may intrude readily. Differential experiences and effects of racism have not changed appreciably historically even though attention has been called to inequities in practice delivery and therapy process, . . . and even though new concepts in treatment delivery have been proposed and partially implemented. (p. 143)

Race has been identified as a major factor in treatment involvement and treatment process. . . . Prevalent differences as associated with race have

Table 1.1   Representative Authors of Publications Reporting Racism in Mental
Health Delivery Systems

Adams (1950)	Lindsey & Paul (1989)
Adams (1970)	Lopez (1989)
Adebimpe (1981, 1982)	Loring & Powell (1988)
Boyd-Franklin (1989)	Malgady, Rogler, & Costantino (1987)
Brantley (1983)	Manderscheid & Barrett (1987)
Butts (1971)	Mass (1967)
Calnek (1970)	Masserman (1960)
Carter (1979, 1983)	Maultsby (1982)
Casimir & Morrison (1993)	Mayo (1974)
Cooper (1973)	Mercer (1984)
Corvin & Wiggins (1989)	Mollica (1990)
d'Ardenne (1993)	Mukherjee, Shukla, Woodle, Rosen, & Olarte
Dreger & Miller (1960)	(1983)
Edwards (1982)	Pavkov, Lewis, & Lyons (1989)
Fernando (1988)	Pinderhughes (1973)
Flaherty & Meagher (1980)	Pinderhughes (1989)
Gardner (1971)	President's Commission on Mental Health (1978)
Garretson (1993)	Rendon (1984)
Garza (1981)	Ridley (1978, 1984, 1985b, 1986c, 1989)
Geller (1988)	Rosado & Elias (1993)
Gerrard (1991)	Rosen & Frank (1962)
Goodman (1973)	Sabshin, Diesenhaus, & Wilkerson (1970)
Grantham (1973)	Sager, Brayboy, & Waxenberg (1972)
Greene (1994)	Shervington (1976)
Grier & Cobbs (1968, 1992)	Snowden & Cheung (1990)
Griffith (1977)	Solomon (1988)
Griffith & Jones (1978)	Solomon (1992)
Gross, Herbert, Knatterrud, & Donner (1969)	Spurlock (1985)
Guthrie (1976)	Stack, Lannon, & Miley (1983)
Hoffman (1993)	Stevenson & Renard (1993)
Hollingshead & Redlich (1958)	Sue (1977)
Jackson (1973, 1976)	Sue (1978)
Jackson, Berkowitz, & Farley (1974)	Sue & Zane (1987)
Jenkins-Hall & Sacco (1991)	Sutton & Kessler (1986)
Jones (1979)	Sykes (1987)
Jones & Gray (1983)	Teichner, Cadden, & Berry (1981)
Jones, Lightfoot, Palmer, Wilkerson, & Williams	Thomas & Sillen (1972)
(1970)	Uba (1982)
Jones & Korchin (1982)	Wade (1993)
Jones & Seagull (1977)	Warren, Jackson, Nugaris, & Farley (1973)
Kadushin (1972)	Watkins, Cowan, & Davis (1975)
Karno (1966)	Willie, Kramer, & Brown (1973)
Katz (1985)	Yamamoto, James, Bloombaum & Hattem (1967)
Korchin (1980)	Yamamoto, James, & Palley (1968)

NOTE: Not every author in this table specifically uses the term *racism*. However, all of the discussions
imply dynamics consistent with the definition of racism proposed in this book.

been found as it pertains to diagnosis disposition, therapy process and outcome. (p. 144)

Although the work of Jackson and many others made it obvious that racism was a continuing problem, little progress was made in dealing with it. Fernando (1988) sheds additional light on the problem of racism in service delivery:

> Discriminatory practices result from ways in which the services are organized —selection procedures, points of comparison for promotion, etc. (in the case of staff) and diagnostic processes, selective criteria for types of treatment, indicators of "dangerousness" etc. (in the case of patients). Racism may have direct advantage for the dominant (white) population in that, for example, the exclusion of black staff from management, and the easing out of black patients from time-consuming types of "sophisticated" treatment modalities or their labelling as (psychiatrically) dangerous, allows white society to continue its dominance. (p. 147)

To see exactly how racism victimizes minority clients, consider some disturbing observations. Compared to White clients, minority clients are more likely to have unfavorable experiences in many aspects of counseling. These include:

- **Diagnosis.** Minority clients tend to receive a misdiagnosis, usually involving more severe psychopathology but occasionally involving less severe psychopathology, more often than is warranted.
- **Staff assignment.** Minority clients tend to be assigned to junior professionals, paraprofessionals, or nonprofessionals for counseling rather than senior and more highly trained professionals.
- **Treatment modality.** Minority clients tend to receive low-cost, less preferred treatment consisting of minimal contact, medication only, or custodial care rather than intensive psychotherapy.
- **Utilization.** Minority clients tend to be represented disproportionately in mental health facilities. Specifically, minority clients are underrepresented in private treatment facilities and overrepresented in public treatment facilities.
- **Treatment duration.** Minority clients show a much higher rate of premature termination and dropout from therapy, or they are confined to much longer inpatient care.
- **Attitudes.** Minority clients report more dissatisfaction and unfavorable impressions regarding treatment.

Factors Contributing to Counselor Racism

Many counselors are well-intentioned professionals who have strong humanistic values. They are motivated to help people who are hurting, and they get personal fulfillment out of their work. Moreover, most counselors place a priority on the ethical principle of client welfare (American Counseling Association [ACA], 1988; American Psychological Association [APA], 1992). If counselors have such lofty human ideals, why is there so much racism in counseling? Part of the answer is that many counselors do not really understand racism. Racism is what people do, regardless of what they think or feel. It is a complex social problem. To really understand racism, careful analysis is needed. The problem is that many counselors cling to oversimplified explanations. The other part of the answer lies in factors that predispose counselors to racist practices. Here are five of these factors.

1. Good Intentions/Bad Interventions

There is a popular cliché, "Good intentions are not good enough." Counselors often assume that their good intentions automatically make them helpful. This implies that only their bad intentions make them unhelpful. As much as good intentions are important, more is needed to be helpful. Consider that, at times, good intentions lead to good results, and at times, they do not. Also consider that bad intentions often lead to bad results, but this is not always true.

Fernando (1988) puts this situation in perspective:

> Racist practices in the context of "bad practice" are easier to detect than those within seemingly "good" practice. Ordinary services carried out by ordinary, honest and decent people can be racist, . . . and it is assumed that "good practice" is automatically non-racist. (pp. 152-153)

Counselors should not be content just to know that their intentions are good. They need to know that what they are doing is indeed helpful. With this in mind, they should also evaluate their interventions. The effectiveness of their interventions matters more than their intentions. If, after taking a good hard look at themselves, they find that they are not as helpful as they thought, they should admit it. Then they should change their behavior so that clients do benefit from counseling. Counselors should update their knowledge and not continue to do things one way just because they always have.

2. Traditional Training

Some counselors assume they are prepared to counsel clients of any background. This assumption is embedded in the philosophy of traditional clinical training. The philosophy holds that existing counseling theories and techniques are appropriate for all people, regardless of their race, ethnicity or culture. Traditionally trained counselors tend to believe they are competent enough to adapt to any differences among clients and serve their best interests (Larson, 1982).

For many years, this generic form of training was the only option available to counselor-trainees. The assumption of "equal applicability" for diverse populations went unchallenged. Therefore, changes in traditional training were deemed unnecessary, and business as usual was the status quo. Over time, strong voices among professional counselors began to question the adequacy of traditional training (Casas, 1984; Ridley, 1985a; Sue & Sue, 1977; Wrenn, 1962). They argued that traditional training did not equip counselors with the necessary skills or competency to be effective with ethnic minority clients. Scientific evidence lent credence to their arguments.

Fortunately, multicultural training has found its way into the curriculum of graduate programs (Ridley, Mendoza, & Kanitz, 1994). However, there remains considerable variability in the quality and content of this training across programs (Hills & Strozier, 1992; Ponterotto & Casas, 1987). Moreover, many clinicians are of a generation of professionals that did not receive multicultural training. Sue and Zane (1987) describe the deficiency of traditional training:

> Most therapists are not familiar with the cultural backgrounds and life-styles of various ethnic-minority groups and have received training primarily developed for Anglo, or mainstream, Americans . . . [and] are often unable to devise culturally appropriate forms of treatment, and ethnic-minority clients frequently find mental health services strange, foreign, or unhelpful. (p. 37)

Traditionally trained counselors should come to terms with the inadequacy of their preparation for service delivery. In some respects, their training is a liability. Counselors who have not had the benefit of multicultural training may be mistaken if they believe they are qualified to counsel minority populations.

3. Cultural Tunnel Vision

Many counselors are ineffective with minority clients because they fail to see the "big picture." They overlook societal factors that influence the behavior and adjustment of these clients. Corey, Corey, and Callanan (1993) describe these counselors as having cultural tunnel vision: "They have had limited cultural experiences, and in many cases they see it as their purpose to teach their clients about their view of the world" (p. 243). The perspective of these authors is in keeping with research on counseling and values, indicating that counselors do not remain value neutral, even when they intend to do so (Kelly, 1990).

Counselors need to broaden their field of vision to include the "realities" of the ethnic minority experience. Jones and Gray (1983) point out that the intrapsychic conflicts of minorities are amplified by external stresses such as racism, economic pressures, and educational disadvantages. Without the broader field of vision and ability to bracket their biases, counselors are prone to expect minority clients to act like them. The so-called YAVIS (young, attractive, verbal, intelligent, successful) is a handy acronym for describing the type of person many counselors prefer as clients (Schofield, 1964).

4. Blaming the Victim

Blaming the victim is the basic human tendency to attribute the cause of victimization to victims themselves while overlooking the real causes. Typically, the process involves shifting the blame from the perpetrator to the victim. Blaming the victim is all too common. According to William Ryan (1971), it "so distorts and disorients the thinking of the average concerned citizen that it becomes a primary barrier to effective social change" (p. xv).

This basic misattribution of blame not only pervades society, it infiltrates the counseling profession. Counselors, however, are scarcely aware of their tendency to blame victims. Ryan (1971) contends that victim blaming "is not a process of intentional distortion although it does serve the class of interests of those who practice it" (p. 11).

In the counseling profession, blaming the victim takes shape in many forms. Much of it is subtle and hides behind the veil of clinical judgment and psychological diagnosis. Sometimes it appears in the labeling of minorities as resistant or untreatable. In whatever form it exists, the profession must discontinue its practice of saying that victims are at fault. The message must be sent loud and clear that it is always wrong to victimize and then blame the victim. Counselors and therapists must realize that their distortions of minority clients are significant causes of racism in the mental health field.

5. Either/Or Thinking

Either/or thinking is the predominant mode of thinking in the Western worldview. This thinking also underlies the conceptual basis of race relations in this country (Dixon, 1971). The either/or framework advances the idea of discrete categories. Everything falls into one category or another. But nothing belongs to more than one category at the same time. The either/or framework has its roots in the logic of Aristotle (1952):

> It is impossible for the same thing at the same time to belong and not to belong to the same thing and in the same respect; and whatever other distinctions we might add to meet dialectical objections, let them be added. This, then, is the most certain of all principles. (p. 68)

The philosophy is based upon several axioms: (a) the law of identity that states that A is A (e.g., an apple is an apple); (b) the law of noncontradiction, that something cannot be both A and Non-A (e.g., something cannot be both an apple and a nonapple); and (c) the law of the excluded middle, that something is either A or Non-A, or neither A nor Non-A (e.g., something is either an apple or a nonapple , or neither an apple nor a nonapple).

Either/or thinking is a legitimate philosophical perspective. However, the theory can be misconstrued, and several false premises derived from it can be erroneously applied to race relations. The first false assumption is the notion of mutual exclusivity. This involves a dichotomizing process. In its extreme form, it assumes that racial groups have nothing in common. Separation of the races is the logical outflow of this assumption. For instance, although segregation is illegal, many Whites do not permit minorities to enter their social space. This separation is depicted as follows:

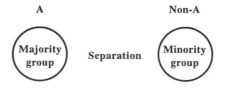

The second assumption is a subtle extension of the first assumption. It assumes group superiority and involves a dehumanizing process. Members of the dominant cultural group devalue members of minority groups, as well as their culture and customs. This assumption—although lacking scientific credibility—allows A to view any deviation from its values as inherently inferior. Tajfel (1978) points out that Whites tend to perceive their values, mode of thinking, and behaviors as superior to those of people they perceive as inferior. A counselor might regard a minority client's value of collectivism as inferior to the value of rugged individualism. Of course, minorities may hold a superior attitude as well. They might regard Whites or other minority groups as inferior. The devaluing process is shown below:

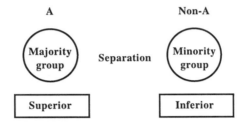

The third assumption is group supremacy. It involves an oppressing process whereby the dominant group dominates and controls the subordinate group. Counselors who regard rugged individualism as a superior value may take further action. They may attribute pathology to minorities who value collectivism. Then they expect these clients to yield their collectivist orientation in favor of the counselor's preferred individualistic orientation. There is research to suggest that therapeutic change is judged as increased conformity to the counselor's values (Kelly, 1990). A's control over Non-A is depicted as follows:

A

Non-A

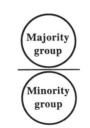

In many respects, either/or thinking is so deeply embedded in Western culture that it goes both unnoticed and unchallenged. The failure to critique either/or thinking also impacts professional behavior. Counselors engage in a host of activities without considering the assumptions underlying them. Although they desire to help minority clients, their own implicit assumptions can interfere with the quality of service delivery.

Chapter Summary

In this opening chapter, minority clients were described as victims of racism in mental health delivery service. Their experiences are often adverse, and documentation of racist practices can be found in earlier writings. The chapter concluded by pointing out five reasons why counselors are susceptible to racism. This discussion should provoke counselors to examine themselves and evaluate their counseling practices. In the next chapter, propositions are set forth that support the definition of racism used in this book.

Note

1. There is a current debate over the use of the terms *victim* and *survivor.* Professionals often speak of persons as survivors of sexual abuse, of trauma, and so on, rather than as victims. I acknowledge this debate but choose not to use this work to attempt to resolve the issue. I prefer to use the term *victim,* because many minorities are still being victimized in mental health delivery systems.

2

Fifteen Propositions

Racism is a polemical topic—one that provokes considerable discussion and controversy. But as Miles (1989) notes, much of the everyday usage of the word *racism* is uncritical. Therefore, discussing this topic with any sense of integrity requires a well-substantiated definition. The definition of racism, like any abstract concept, should rest on a set of constituent propositions: statements that are affirming of a concept. Propositions are conceptual building blocks. They function much like a foundation that supports the weight of a building.

It follows that the strength of a concept, much like the structural integrity of a building, depends on carefully formulated propositions. Any concept that does not have a sturdy foundation will eventually collapse under its own unsupported weight. A rigorous intellectual test would only hasten its demise. What is disturbing is that few professionals stop to reflect on their propositions. All too often, their propositions are implicit. Unidentified and unexamined, this condition of propositions makes a concept especially vulnerable to collapse.

This chapter lays the groundwork for defining and elaborating on racism. The concept needs a crisp and accurate definition. To achieve this end, 15 supporting propositions are critically examined. This examination should channel the reader's thinking and dispel unfounded notions about racism.

16

Propositions

Proposition 1: Racism Is Reflected in Human Behavior

The most important thing to say about racism is that it is behavior—what a person actually does. Any definition that excludes this basic premise is incomplete. It is more accurate to say that racism involves motor behavior, technically known as operant behavior. This class of behavior is voluntary. Running, typing, and washing windows are operant behaviors. These are distinguished from respondent behaviors, such as eye blinks and knee jerks, which are involuntary. This proposition implies that people can voluntarily control their racist behavior. Even the most blatant bigots, when made aware of their racism, can change. They have to first decide that this is what they want to do.

Several features characterize behavior. First, behavior is *observable.* A counselor can be observed conducting an intake interview or writing a psychological report. This characteristic distinguishes behavior from non-behavior, which cannot be observed. Unless people in the behavior setting have a visual disability or a physical barrier blocks their field of vision, they can readily observe racist behavior.

Second, behavior is *repeatable.* Once a behavior has occurred, it can reoccur. If you learn to ride a bicycle, you can repeat cycling behavior. The exception is when a physical limitation or outside force interferes with the behavior. A cyclist who breaks a leg or rides into a hurricane probably cannot continue cycling. If not for these types of interferences, the cyclist could more than likely repeat the behavior. Any act of racism can be a onetime event or recurring behavior. This depends upon the degree of freedom people have to continue their racist behavior and whether or not they choose it.

Third, behavior is *measurable.* Astute observers can count the frequency of a behavior. All they need to do is to decide what behavior they want to measure and then place themselves in a position where observation is possible. If they could observe a therapy session, they might count a psychologist's open-ended questions, reflections of feelings, paraphrases, and interpretations. If a hidden camera were installed in the counseling office, the counselor's behavior could be measured unobtrusively.

Proposition 2: Racism Is Not Racial Prejudice

There are numerous terms and phrases used to describe race-related dynamics. Racism and racial prejudice are two such widely used concepts.

Often they are used interchangeably, but this interchange creates confusion. Although both of these concepts involve some form of bias, they are different dynamics. The confusion over terminology is a major problem. It hinders efforts to understand and resolve racial tensions.

Prejudice is a preconceived judgment or opinion without justification or sufficient knowledge (Axelson, 1993). This predisposition can be positive or negative. A counselor may have a prejudice for YAVIS (young, attractive, verbal, intelligent, successful) clients (Schofield, 1964) and against religious fundamentalists, lumping members of each group together without considering the merits of each individual. Locke (1992) notes that everyone uses some prior knowledge in an urgency to categorize people, implying that everyone is prejudiced in one way or another.

Racial prejudice usually carries a negative connotation. Schaefer (1988) defines racial prejudice as negative attitudes, thoughts, and beliefs about an entire category of people. Along similar lines, Davis (1978) defines racial prejudice as an attitude expressing unfavorable feelings and behavioral intentions toward a group or its individual members. He includes the phrase "behavioral intentions" in his definition. Behavioral intentions, however, are not actual behaviors. They are dispositions toward behaving in certain ways.

Racism always involves harmful behavior, whereas racial prejudice involves only negative attitudes, beliefs, and intentions. Herein lies the major difference between these two phenomena. Racism is behavioral, and prejudice is dispositional.

**Proposition 3:   Although Racial Prejudice Involves Unfavorable Attitudes
and Intentions, It Does Not Necessarily Translate Into Racism**

It is widely held that to be a racist, one must be prejudiced. According to Lum (1992), there is a misconception that prejudice always precedes racism. Some social scientists, such as Leigh (1984), propagate this point of view, but their logic has a flaw. This conventional point of view assumes a causal relationship in which prejudice is the presumed underlying cause and racism is the effect. This assumed relationship is illustrated as follows:

$$\textbf{CAUSE} \longrightarrow \textbf{EFFECT}$$

Prejudice	**Racism**
Nonprejudice	**Nonracism**

There is an assumed corollary in this logic. Without the presence of prejudice, there can be no racism. What this means is that people who are not prejudiced do not behave as racists. Implicit here is the more deeply embedded assumption that nonracists do not have harmful behavioral intentions.

This argument sounds logical. Devious acts are typically associated with people who have moral, ethical, or character flaws. Well-known deviants such as Jeffrey Dahmer and the Night Stalker reinforce the belief that only bad people do bad deeds. But well-intentioned people sometimes harm others. They may bring harm to others for a variety of reasons. For example, they may be misinformed or unaware of the harmful consequences of their behavior. Their ignorance does not make the consequences of their actions any less detrimental.

Smedes (1984) observes that people hurt others with their good intentions:

> Sometimes people hurt us even when they mean to do us good. Their well-meant plans go awry, maybe through other people's knavery, maybe by their own bungling. No matter how, what they do to help us turns out to hurt us. (p. 11)

The contribution of Ignaz Semmelweiss, the so-called "savior of mothers," dramatizes the seriousness of unintentional harm. In 1847, he noticed that women in Vienna who gave birth at home had a much lower mortality rate than women who delivered in the hospital. This problem interested Semmelweiss. He went on to discover that the fatal puerperal infection was transmitted by the hands of obstetricians examining women during labor. Although 19th century medical practice seems primitive when measured against modern standards, Semmelweiss's discovery underscores an important reality: Professionals with the best of intentions can be dangerous. Their harmful behavior may not necessarily result from malicious intent.

Conversely, people with malicious intentions are not necessarily harmful. Their potential to harm others may be prevented by a more powerful force—sometimes the behavioral sanctions enforced by society or sometimes the more powerful counteractions of the intended victim. What this means is that, even though someone is prejudiced, he or she may temporarily refrain or be restrained from acting like a racist.

Proposition 4: Anyone Can Be a Racist, Including Members of Racial Minority Groups

There are widely held stereotypes of the racist, such as a White supremacist or an ignorant bigot. Ku Klux Klan members, skinheads, and Archie Bunker fit these stereotypes. Some of the most heinous acts of racism are indeed committed by members of hate groups, and many of their notorious deeds are well-publicized. Many people believe that to be a racist one has to match one of these profiles.

Are White bigots really the only ones responsible for racism? Consider that minorities, at times, victimize other minorities. Racism practiced by minorities is real—as real as incest, where the victim and perpetrator are both members of the same family. The racist behavior of one minority toward another may be intentional, or it may be unintentional. But racism practiced by members of minority groups does not end there. Minorities can also behave like racists toward Whites. A gang of Black youths can assault an unsuspecting White passerby in a city park. Although it may not be popular to say that minorities can be racists, counselors should never discount anyone as a racist simply because of the person's skin color. If race is the basis for deciding who is a racist, the more important issue—that it is actions that make a racist—gets discounted. More daunting would be the hindrance this poses to broadscale elimination of racism.

Proposition 5: The Criteria for Determining Racism Lie in the Consequences of the Behavior, Not the Causes

Intentions should not be used as the criteria for determining whether or not a behavior is racist. As previously noted, racial prejudice does not always cause racism. Even when racism is motivated by prejudice, the person's motivations still do not indicate if the behavior is racist. This is not to discount the occurrence of visible bigotry and racially motivated acts of violence and vandalism. Behavioral intentions are valuable areas to explore. They convey a great deal about why people behave as they do. Yet intentions are not the real problem. Taking a cue from Semmelweiss, it may be more beneficial to focus attention on the consequences of behavior.

To better evaluate racism, a topology for the classification of behavior is proposed. (See Figure 2.1.) The consequences of behavior can be divided into two categories: adverse and nonadverse. People are either victimized by the behaviors of others, or they are not victimized. Motivations underlying the behavior also can be placed into two categories: prejudiced and nonprejudiced. People either negatively judge others without justification, or they do not.

Combinations of the two categories of behavioral consequences and the underlying motivation yield four possible types of individuals: (a) a prejudiced person who is racist, (b) a prejudiced person who is not racist,

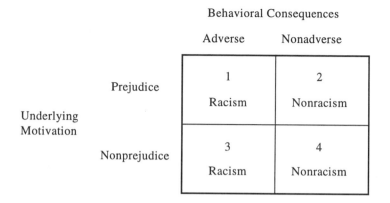

Figure 2.1. Behavior Typology for Classifying Racism and Nonracism

(c) a nonprejudiced person who is racist, and (d) a nonprejudiced person who is not racist. According to this typology, racism is determined by the adverse consequences of a person's behavior. Whether or not the racist is prejudiced is of secondary importance. For it is possible to not be prejudiced and yet act like a racist unintentionally. A useful rule for determining racism is to look at behavior consequences first and motivation second. Regardless of a counselor's motivation, actual clinical behavior is what affects a client.

Proposition 6: A Person Needs Power to Behave Like a Racist

It takes more than malicious intent to behave like a racist. Some people are too powerless to harm others. Even the imperial wizard of the Ku Klux Klan cannot behave like a racist if he is stripped of his power. He may hate Blacks and people of Semitic backgrounds, but the imperial wizard cannot personally carry out hate crimes if he becomes severely disabled.

It takes power to behave like a racist. Power is the ability to control ourselves and others (Leigh, 1984). Counselors, for example, control access to goals that are of interest to minority clients. They select treatments, make diagnoses, and refer clients to other agencies. These actions can have far-reaching consequences. If counselors are misguided in their actions, tremendous harm can be done.

Minorities in the general society have considerably less power than Whites. In the mental health field, the power imbalance is reflected in the tremendous underrepresentation of ethnic minorities among practicing professionals (Ridley, 1985a). For example, ethnic minorities represent just under 7% of all psychologists, a percentage that has remained constant for more than a decade (Tomes, 1994). White professionals overwhelmingly make up the largest group of service providers. Because racism is so pervasive in mental health delivery systems, it follows that White professionals own a large share of the problem. In testimony before a House subcommittee, Esteban Olmedo stated that a shortage of ethnic-minority mental health professionals is one of the major obstacles to quality service for disadvantaged and minority clients (Moses-Zirkes, 1993).

Proposition 7: Failing to Combat Racism Is Racism

Most discussions of racism focus on direct and deliberate acts of the racist. Consider another perspective—indirect racism. Suppose one has the ability to rescue a drowning child but does nothing. The consequence of inaction could be fatal. Inaction, in fact, could lead to the same consequence as when a child is pushed into deep water. The child drowns.

Racism—like the drowning of a child—can occur directly through action or indirectly through inaction. In the former situation, the person does something to bring about the fatal consequence. In the latter situation, the person does nothing, but doing nothing results in the same fatal consequence. In both situations, the person has the ability to influence the outcome.

Direct forms of racism, such as violence and vandalism, are usually easy to challenge for what they are. Indirect forms of racism, on the other hand, are more elusive. But the failure to combat racism in any form is not just a simple act of racism; it is a perpetuation of racism, especially when the bystander has the power to prevent it. A well-known adage popularized during the civil rights movement of the 1950s and 1960s aptly describes those who participate in indirect racism: "If you are not a part of the solution, you are part of the problem."

Counselors cannot easily dismiss their responsibility in combating racism. Even counselors who are not bigots participate in a larger system that victimizes minorities. Using ineffectual interventions, misdiagnosing clients, and imposing biased cultural expectations are among the many ways minorities are victimized in counseling. No client deserves this type of mistreatment. Certainly, mental health professionals face a great challenge. But if they do not at least try to stop racism, they actually behave in a racist manner by allowing it to continue.

Proposition 8: Although Racism Is Observable, Racist Behavior Is Not Always Observed

Behavior is either public or private. Observers can usually see public behavior, but private behavior, for the most part, cannot be seen. Private behavior typically occurs behind the scenes and out of the viewing range of other people. In the privacy of an office, a counselor can misinterpret test data and case history information. The counselor can write the misinterpretation up in a psychological report without anyone ever examining the original source of data. This unobserved activity can have detrimental consequences.

Racism—whether observed or not—is still racism. It brings harm to its victims. Racism in private, however, poses an additional threat. It is more difficult to change than racism in public. People usually cannot change what they do not know exists, and they usually do not know something exists unless they first see it. Many acts of racism occur in private, making these behaviors unavailable for public scrutiny. This situation interferes with efforts to eliminate racism. Change agents can only infer the existence of unobserved racism, unless they are astute enough to recognize its consequences.

Proposition 9: Racism Is Learned, the Same Way Any Operant Behavior Is Learned

Racist behavior is different from nonracist behavior in one way—its impact on the victim and the larger social community. In every other respect, these two kinds of behaviors are fundamentally alike. Both reflect the individual's learning history, and both are based upon the same general principles of learning. Moreover, both belong to the operant class of behavior.

Learning can be defined as "a relatively permanent change in potential performance or behavior as a result of experience" (Mancucella, 1985, p. 1). This definition includes two critical elements. The word *potential* indicates that learned behavior is not always manifested. Under certain conditions, a more powerful force may interfere with the display of the learned behavior. A novice counselor, taking a traditional textbook approach and using outdated norms, may conclude that a minority student who has marginal test scores is intellectually deficient. A competent supervisor may overrule the evaluation, recognizing that the counselor has an antiquated understanding of assessment.

Second, nonlearning influences on behavior are excluded from the definition. Not all changes in behavior are the result of learning. Some changes are temporary, such as when a person's behavior is influenced by drugs or fatigue. Hence the phrase *relatively permanent* is used. Other changes are permanent, resulting from physical factors such as the aging process and illness. Thus the word *experience* has been included in the definition.

Proposition 10: Because Racism Is Operant Behavior, It Can Be Changed

Eliminating racism is a major social concern. Most people agree that racism is wrong. It is a violation of human rights. Racism is also inconsistent with the democratic principles upon which this country was founded. But agreeing that racism is wrong and actually changing this social problem are two different matters.

Attempts to eliminate racism must be rooted in a basic understanding of the psychology of behavior. No one is *born* a racist, because racism is learned like any operant behavior. This implies that no one has to behave as a racist.

The question to ask is not "Can racism be changed?" It can. There are more important questions. "How can racism be changed?" and "Will racism be changed?" To answer these questions, counselors need to understand the laws of behavior change and make a commitment to the process of change. Overcoming racism in counseling depends upon the willingness of counselors to learn and practice new patterns of behavior.

Proposition 11: Consciousness Raising Is an Inadequate Method of Combating Racism

Spurred by the civil rights and women's movements, society has witnessed a tremendous emphasis on consciousness raising. During the past several decades, numerous efforts have been initiated to promote the equality of minorities and women. These attempts have employed the power of persuasion, a clarification of the injustices in society, and an appeal to morality. Despite having a persuasive message, consciousness raising yields disappointing results. Major inequities continue to exist.

Proponents of consciousness raising correctly recognize the problem of inequality, but they flounder as change agents. They tend to aim their change efforts at some presumed underlying cause rather than racist behavior itself. Of course, they should examine behavioral intentions such as prejudice. But their priority should be changing problem behavior. This is what proponents of consciousness raising often overlook and why they fail.

Moreover, even when behavior change is proposed, these proponents often describe the behavior in the most general terms. They might say that counselors need to become culturally sensitive. Yet they provide no clue as to what it means to be culturally sensitive and how this differs from being culturally insensitive. Although they advocate change, proponents of consciousness raising offer vague guidelines as to how improved counselors should behave.

Proposition 12: To Change Racism, Begin by Identifying Specific Behaviors as Racist

As long as counselors are unaware of the harmful effects of their behavior, they probably will not see the need to change. Equitable and fair treatment of minorities requires that counselors determine whether or not their behavior is racist. To accomplish this task, they should attempt to see which category their behavior fits in the proposed behavior typology.

Counselors may classify their behavior as either racist or nonracist. In attempting to classify their behavior or the behavior of others, they may make any of four possible decisions: correctly identifying behavior as racism, correctly identifying behavior as nonracism, incorrectly identifying behavior as racism, and incorrectly identifying behavior as nonracism.

Two of these decisions are correct, and two are incorrect. Unfortunately, people do not always recognize racism when they see it. Their misidentification stems from having an inadequate definition of racism and not knowing the appropriate criteria for judging behavior. Changing racism requires the identification of specific behaviors of individuals. Unless counselors take this course of action, they are not likely to overcome their racism.

Proposition 13: Racism Tends to Resist Change

Behavior change is seldom automatic. Human beings are creatures of habit. Their patterns of behavior are well-established and backed up by a long history of reinforcement. Attempts to change racism—like attempts to change any well-established behavior—are typically met with resistance.

The encounter with resistance has two important implications. Changing racist behavior is a serious challenge. It demands careful attention and commitment based on the scientific principles of behavior change. Counselors must meet this challenge head-on if they are to overcome racism in counseling and therapy. Second, counselors can overcome their racism. They can acquire empowering behaviors, helping themselves to better serve minority clients.

Proposition 14: To Prevent a Relapse Into Racism, Nonracist Behaviors and Fair Practices Must Be Acquired, Reinforced, and Carefully Monitored

Overcoming racism is one accomplishment. Maintaining equitable practices and preventing the recurrence of racism is another. The science of human behavior distinguishes behavioral assets from behavioral deficits. Behavioral assets are socially appropriate and self-enhancing behaviors. Behavioral deficits are socially inappropriate and self-destructive behaviors. Attributing pathology to minority clients who exhibit mannerisms unfamiliar to a counselor could be a behavioral deficit. But just stopping this behavior does not mean the counselor has developed a behavioral asset. The counselor needs to acquire skills in multicultural assessment.

One of the best ways to prevent relapse into racism is to reinforce behaviors that take the place of racist behaviors. Two competing behaviors cannot coexist simultaneously. Counselors cannot simultaneously engage in racist behavior and nonracist behavior. In the language of behaviorism, preventing relapse involves the differential reinforcement of other behavior (DRO). Applied to this discussion, it involves the reinforcement of equitable practices that are incompatible with racist practices. As an example, if counselors are reinforced for conducting good multicultural assessments, they will not do poor assessments. To ensure long-lasting equitable treatment, counselors need clear descriptions of helpful behaviors, methods of evaluating the consequences of these behaviors, and methods for observing and measuring the frequency of these behaviors. Without an effective system of monitoring, chances are that counselors will drift back into racist practices.

Proposition 15: Combating Racism in Counseling Is the Responsibility of Every Mental Health Professional

Earlier in this chapter, it was noted that no race has a monopoly on racism. Anyone is capable of behaving as a racist. Moreover, racism has a long and pervasive history in mental health delivery service. Therefore, all counselors—regardless of race—should be involved in combating their own racism and the racism of other professionals. This stance echoes the position taken by Ponterotto and Pedersen (1993), who also conclude that racism and prejudice transcend all peoples. If racism is to be eliminated in mental health systems, counselors must begin to take personal responsibility for the way things are, rather than exclaiming, "It's not my problem."

It could be argued that counteracting racism in counseling ought to be an ethical mandate. Current ethical standards are ineffectual in promoting the welfare of minority consumers. These standards have several short-comings (Ridley, Mendoza, & Kanitz, 1994). They fail to reflect the state of knowledge regarding diversity. They show a bias toward Eurocentric values, and they emphasize the prevention of harm but not the provision of benefits to minorities. Counselors should explore these issues and search for ways to make professional ethics more responsive to minority consumers.

Chapter Summary

Fifteen propositions support the concept of racism used in this book. Most prominent among them is the fact that racism is operant behavior. Racism is what people do, which means it can be observed, repeated, and measured. The other propositions emanate from this central theme. Building on the foundation developed in Chapters 1 and 2, Chapter 3 elaborates on the definition of racism used in this book.

3

What Is Racism?

Many definitions of racism have been proposed. One only has to read several discussions on the topic to discover the variety of ways the term is defined. Even social scientists and human relations experts seldom agree on a uniform definition. In fact, they often contradict each other. This confuses the average person. Probably, the contraditions are hazardous to advances in racial understanding.

This chapter attempts to erase the confusion surrounding racism. It is intended to move the reader beyond polemic by proposing a coherent definition of the term. The definition is grounded in the 15 propositions described in Chapter 2. After defining racism, a behavioral model that separates the construct into its various component behaviors is presented.

Racism Defined

Racism is any behavior or pattern of behavior that tends to systematically deny access to opportunities or privileges to members of one racial group while perpetuating access to opportunities and privileges to members of another racial group (Ridley, 1989; Taborn, personal communication, February, 1977).[1] This definition consists of five key features: a variety of behaviors, systematic behavior, preferential treatment, inequitable outcomes, and nonrandom victimization. Explanation of each of these features should help the reader gain a better understanding of racism.

Many Possible Behaviors

When most people think about racism, they envision sensational and blatant acts of bigotry. They may recall images of angry mobs of White people on television, attacking civil rights demonstrators in peaceful protest, or hooded Klansmen burning crosses. People seldom see themselves as racists because their behaviors do not fit these descriptions. But this is a misperception. Racism is more—actually much more—than a few notorious acts of violence. Racism involves a wide variety of behaviors, many of which are not usually thought of as racism.

Counselors engage in numerous professional behaviors. Table 3.1 outlines general categories and specific behaviors of counselors. Among their many behaviors, counselors ask probing questions, take case notes, interpret client defenses, provide feedback, and give homework assignments. These are only a few of the types of behavior falling under the rubric of counseling. This audit shows the immense possibilities for racism in the counseling profession. Suppose a counselor misinterprets an Asian client's deference. The client may be showing respect for authority, but the counselor may view the client as passive. In the chapters that follow, many examples of racism in counseling will be discussed.

The audit makes another revelation. Not every behavior of a counselor, even the most blatantly racist, is racism. The racism of most counselors occurs on a small scale compared to their total repertoire of professional behaviors. But even minuscule amounts of racism can have harmful consequences. In the aggregate, across many counselors, racism exists in incredible magnitude. Counselors should strive to have not simply fewer racist behaviors, but no racism in their behavior repertoire.

Systematic Behavior

Racism does not exist in a vacuum. It operates in larger social contexts where people interact with one another. General systems theory is useful for explaining human behavior. The theory is particularly helpful in demonstrating racism as a problem of social systems. A system is a pattern of relationships that prevails over time. Katz and Kahn (1978), in their classic work on organizations, provide an insightful description of social systems:

Table 3.1   Behavior Repertoire of Mental Health Professionals

Direct Service Delivery

Counseling	Prescribing medication
Assessing and diagnosing	Terminating treatment
Writing case notes	Interpreting test data
Writing psychological reports	Consulting
Making referrals	Prevention

Training

Teaching	Evaluating
Conducting workshops	Supervising
Writing instructional material	

Administration

Delegating	Hiring
Organizing	Firing
Planning	Budgeting
Monitoring	Scheduling appointments

Policy Making

Evaluating proposals for change
Legislating policy
Lobbying

Research and Scholarly Activity

Describing the psychology of ethnic minorities
Hypothesis testing
Designing research
Reviewing literature
Selecting instrumentation for measurement
Interpreting data
Writing proposals for research grants

All social systems, including organizations, consist of the patterned activities of a number of individuals. Moreover, these patterned activities are complementary or interdependent with respect to some common output or outcome; they are repeated, relatively enduring, and bounded in space and time. If the activity pattern occurs only once or at unpredictable intervals, we could not speak of an organization. The stability or recurrence of activities can be examined in relation to the energetic input into the system, the transformation of energies within the system, and the resulting product or energic output. (p. 20)

Three important characteristics of open systems are embedded in this definition, and these are relevant to understanding racism. Figure 3.1

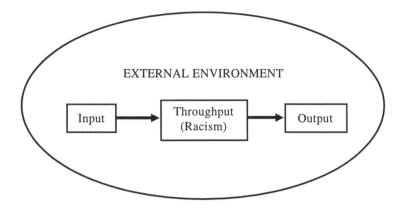

Figure 3.1. Racism as Social Systems Behavior

depicts racism as social systems behavior, consisting of input, throughput, and output.[2]

1. *Input.* Open systems import energy in some form from the external environment. Katz and Kahn (1978) point out how the human body takes in oxygen from the air and food from the external world. To survive, social systems must similarly draw renewed supplies of energy from the larger external environment. Because no social system is self-sufficient or self-contained, the survival of racism depends upon inputs such as money, personnel, attitudes, and mental paradigms. For example, government money may be spent on programs that are disempowering and foster dependency among minorities. Professionals may enter the mental health field with the attitude that minority issues are not important. Even minority clients may enter the sanctum of the counseling session with great suspicion. If clinicians fail to deal constructively with these types of input, the consequences are almost certain to be negative.

2. *Throughput.* Surviving open systems transform their energetic input. Katz and Kahn (1978) point out how the human body converts starch and sugar into heat and action. Social systems create products, convert materials, change people, or offer services. Essentially, social systems change their inputs into qualitatively different outputs. Racism may be viewed as a process of systemic transformation—behavior and patterns of behavior transforming minority clients into victims. In counseling, the micro-

interaction between counselor and client is where much of the throughput occurs. In addition to direct service delivery, counselors engage in training, administration, policy making, and research and scholarly activity. All of these are system behaviors. Depending upon their consequences, any counselor behavior in these categories may be racist.

3. *Output.* Open systems export products—the transformed inputs—into the environment. Katz and Kahn (1978) point out how the human body exports carbon dioxide from the lungs. Similarly, racist outcomes are linked to a system's input and throughput. When minority consumers leave the mental health system prematurely, unhelped, misdiagnosed, or disenchanted, these are the outputs of systemic behavior.

Input, throughput, and output suggest that racism is a function of social systems. Just like the numerous survival activities of the human body, racism is reinforced by larger social systems. Without this support and reinforcement, racism could not exist. Therefore, efforts to change racism —even the isolated behavior of individuals—must include a systems perspective.

Preferential Treatment

In a fair system, everyone has equal opportunity. No one is unfairly advantaged or disadvantaged. Racism, however, involves preferential treatment. Members of the preferred group have an unfair advantage over members of the nonpreferred group. Suppose two 15-year-old boys agree to a wrestling match. The boys are of equal height, weight, strength, and intelligence. One boy has never wrestled. The other boy, however, has trained for a year under an Olympic team wrestling coach. Despite the many similarities between the two boys, there is one important difference between them. One boy is placed in an advantageous position over the other.

In the mental health system, Whites have an advantage over minorities. As an example, Leong (1992) addresses the disadvantage Asians sometimes encounter in group counseling:

> In many Asian cultures, there is a strong cultural value that involves humility and modesty in social interactions. This value is often expressed in the form of deferential behavior and not drawing excessive attention to oneself and one's personal concerns. . . . The group climate of open and free self-expression may then be experienced by these Asian Americans as an uncomfortable and culturally alien demand. (p. 219)

Leong (1992) argues that this conflict in values contributes to premature termination among Asians. It could be surmised that White clients are in a more advantageous position than Asian clients in group counseling. Unless group counselors are cross-culturally competent, they are not likely to facilitate the group experience in ways that maximally benefit Asian clients. Racism denies equal access to opportunities and privileges to one race while perpetuating these to another race. No group of people deserves an unfair advantage or disadvantage.

Inequitable Outcomes

Racism typically confers benefits to members of the majority group but not members of minority groups. The benefits may be psychological, social, economic, material, or political. As a result, Whites consistently find themselves in a one-up position over minorities. The inequitable outcomes of racism can be illustrated in this way:

$$\text{Racism} \quad \rightarrow \quad \frac{\text{Majority group}}{\text{Minority Group}}$$

Consistent inequitable outcomes can be easily found in the mental health field. Chapter 1 pointed out inequitable outcomes found in the areas of diagnosis, staff assignment, treatment modality, utilization, treatment duration, and attitudes toward treatment. Rogler (1993) states that the *Diagnostic and Statistical Manual of Mental Disorders (DSM-III-R)* gives scant attention to the significance of culture. Yet the manual is more widely used cross-nationally than any other system for classifying mental illnesses. According to Rogler (1993), the current taxonomy leads to diagnostic errors, stemming from either the neglect of culture or misconceptions about culture. With such a powerful tool of the mental health system, it is easy to see why minorities find themselves in the one-down position. Figure 3.3 depicts the mental health system as racist, resulting in inequitable outcomes.

The inequitable outcomes found in Figure 3.2 are reminiscent of those illustrated in Chapter 1. This could imply that racism is tied inextricably to either/or thinking, which is deeply embedded in our culture. Professional paradigms and models often categorize people, favoring persons whose behaviors are consistent with traditional Western values. These paradigms may very well contribute to unintentional racist outcomes, because many mental health workers are committed to professional business as usual.

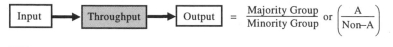

 Represents the systematic transformation of minority clients into victims

Figure 3.2. Mental Health System as Racist

Nonrandom Victimization

It is one thing to be a victim: just another statistic. It is despicable when members of a racial group are repeatedly victimized. One may think that the adverse experiences of ethnic minorities in counseling are due to chance occurrence—that these are random events. This point of view implies that neither the victim (i.e., the ethnic minority client) or the social setting (i.e., the counseling office or clinic) is responsible for the repeated difficulties minorities have in counseling. Probability theory strongly suggests the presence of an influencing dynamic.

Consider a probability experiment. A barrel contains 100 balls, 50 of which are black and 50 of which are white. Each ball is drawn individually and not replaced. Successive drawings are made, without replacement, until all of the balls are drawn. In addition, the first 25 balls selected are tossed into the trash.

Assuming that the balls are thoroughly mixed (unbiased), a probability of 1/100 is assigned to the selection of each ball. Each ball has an equal chance of being selected. Although 100 possible outcomes exist, predicting when a particular ball will be selected is impossible. During the experiment, an interesting observation is made. The first 25 balls selected are black. They are thrown away. Thus all of the white balls but only half of the black balls are retained. The experimenter could conclude that white balls are luckier than black balls.

The favorable selection of white balls over black balls is certainly possible. According to the laws of chance, however, these experimental outcomes are improbable. With that many selections, there should be a fairly proportionate number of black and white balls selected. The chance occurrence or recurrence of an event or set of events in a given sample space (situation) is measured by the ratio of the number of cases or alternatives favorable to the event to the total number of cases or alternatives. It is statistically improbable that only the black balls but not white balls are trashed, all things being equal. But this is precisely the problem.

All things probably are not equal. The most likely explanation is that the favorable selection of white balls is due to outside influences.

In an equitable system, the recurring victimization of minority clients is improbable. When minority clients repeatedly drop out prematurely, get assigned to junior professionals, or receive inaccurate diagnoses, it is difficult to explain these outcomes as chance occurrence. Systematic influence—the behavior operative in the mental health delivery system—is a more plausible explanation. As such, racism could be described as nonrandom victimization: the systematic denial of access to opportunities and privileges.

I have been asked on various occasions, "Isn't it true that White clients are also victimized in counseling?" My answer is an unqualified yes. They may be mistreated by an incompetent counselor, and the fact of their victimization is no less serious than the victimization of minorities. But these events tend to be random. The victimization of minority clients is more often due to racism, which is both nonrandom and predictable.

A Behavioral Model[3]

To further clarify the dynamics of racism, a behavioral model is proposed. The model is based upon the proposed definition and categorizes racism into its essential component behaviors. Each of the behavioral categories is a type or level of racism. No category of behavior in the model represents racism exclusively. The model is outlined as follows:

I. Individual Racism
   A. Overt (always intentional)
   B. Covert
      1. Intentional
      2. Unintentional

II. Institutional Racism
   A. Overt (always intentional)
   B. Covert
      1. Intentional
      2. Unintentional

The model classifies racism into two major behavioral categories: individual and institutional. Individual racism involves the adverse behavior of one person or small group of people. A waitress who refuses to serve a minority customer in a restaurant is exhibiting individual racism. Institutional racism involves the adverse behavior of organizations or institutions (Sedlacek & Brooks, 1976). The Jim Crow laws in the South, which imposed a variety of limitations on Black access to public accommodations, including the requirement that they sit at the back of buses, represented institutional practices of racism.

The major categories of racism can be subdivided into smaller units of behavior. Overt racism, which may be either individual or institutional, is always intentional. Overt racist behavior implies intentionality on the part of the perpetrator, leaving no room for doubt about the racist's underlying motive. When a Black man is lynched, malicious intent is unmistakably implied by the behavior.

Covert racism, on the other hand, is more subtle. It is similar to overt racism in that it is reflected in the behavior of either individuals or institutions, and the criterion making it racist is its consequences. In covert racism, unlike overt racism, the motives underlying the behavior are hidden. Others are left to guess or hypothesize about the motive of the covert racist. The only person who really knows the underlying motive is the person who performs the racist behavior. In fact, some racists are skillful in hiding or masking their motives. They might be the first to say, "There isn't a racist bone in my body!" They may even attempt to present themselves as behaving out of beneficence toward the victim.

Covert acts of racism may be either intentional or unintentional. Intentional covert racism involves malicious intent. The behaviors of intentional racists are consistent with their motives, even though others may be unable to identify those motives. Unintentional covert racism involves nonmaleficence. The behaviors of unintentional racists result in consequences that are often contradictory to their motives. Examples of the various types of racism in mental health delivery systems are found in Table 3.2.

Unintentional Racism:
An Insidious Form of Victimization

It should now be obvious to the reader that racism is a complex social problem. It has many faces. Solutions to racism cannot be proposed until its definition and component behaviors are understood. Whether the behavior is individual or institutional, overt or covert, intentional or unintentional, it is racism if the result is systematic victimization.

In general, overt forms of racism are the easiest to identify. This means that these are also the easiest to overcome. Today overt racism is illegal.

Table 3.2 Examples of Racism in Mental Health Delivery Systems

	Individual Racism	*Institutional Racism*
Overt	A therapist who believes that ethnic minorities are inferior and on this basis refuses to accept them as clients[a]	A mental health agency that openly denies treatment to ethnic minority clientele[a]
Covert Intentional	A senior psychologist who assigns a minority client to an intern because of social discomfort but claims to have a schedule overload	A mental health agency that deliberately sets fees above the affordable range of most ethnic minority clients, thus excluding them from treatment
Unintentional	A therapist, functioning under the illusion of color blindness, who erroneously diagnoses pathology	A mental health agency that routinely uses standardized psychological tests without consideration of subcultural group differences and biases in test construction and interpretation

SOURCE: Ridley, C. R. (1989). Racism in counseling as an adversive behavioral process. In P. B. Pederson, J. G. Draguns, W. J. Lonner, & J. E. Trimble (Eds.), *Counseling across cultures* (3rd ed.) (pp. 55-77). Honolulu: University of Hawaii Press. Reprinted by permission.
NOTE: a. These practices are now illegal according to federal civil rights legislation.

For example, Title VII of the 1964 Civil Rights Act prohibits discrimination in hiring, placement, and promotion on the basis of race, color, sex, religion, ethnic background, or national origin. To a large extent, the legal system can monitor and enforce these practices. Although overt racism has not been totally eradicated, society has come a long way in reducing the incidence of overt racist practices.

But what about other forms of racism? There is evidence that more subtle forms of racism have replaced blatant discrimination (Dovidio & Gaertner, 1986). Sedlacek and Brooks (1976) went a step further, pointing out that most racism is unknowing or unintentional:

> Most people do not know enough about the sources or effects of their behavior to realize how it damages someone of another race. It is even more destructive as a collective action of the majority society. For instance, if a white belongs to an organization that excludes blacks, formally or informally, then he or she is lending support to a racist organization, whether or not he or she realizes it or has the best intentions. The consequences are that blacks can't get in. (p. 43)

Unintentional behavior is perhaps the most insidious form of racism. Unintentional racists are unaware of the harmful consequences of their behavior. They may be well-intentioned, and on the surface, their behavior may appear to be responsible. Because individuals, groups, or institutions that engage in unintentional racism do not wish to do harm, it is difficult to get them to see themselves as racists. They are more likely to deny their racism. What they need to realize is that it is not necessarily the person wearing the white sheet and carrying a torch who poses the greatest threat. Unintentional racists, cloaked in their sincerity and desire to do good, often do some of the greatest harm. Certainly, overt racism is not completely eradicated. Sometimes counselors do harm minority clients with their bad intentions. But the position taken by Dovidio and Gaertner (1986) is probably on target. Covert racism is now the more pervasive problem. The major challenge facing counselors is to overcome unintentional racism and provide more equitable service delivery.

Therapist Inaction as Racism

Therapist inaction—the behaviors of omission—should be highlighted. Some professionals are so frightened of doing the wrong thing that they refuse to do or say anything. They attempt to escape racism by "doing nothing" but end up perpetuating the problem they seek to avoid. One version of inaction is when White professionals defer responsibility to minority professionals. They assume that minority professionals are the exclusive experts on treating minority clients. Not only is this avoidance behavior irresponsible, it places an unfair burden on minority profession-als. Ironically, placing this heavy burden on minority professionals is yet another act of racism.

Therapist inaction is more than a problem of White professionals. Some minority professionals are so confident in "doing the right thing" that they are closed-minded. In an attempt to attack racism, they end up "doing the wrong thing." They assume that they understand the dynamics of racism when they may not. Another version of inaction is when minority profes-sionals posture as experts on treating minority clients. However, they may avoid examining their own racism, or they may not take the time to become competent in dealing with minority issues.

Most professionals will encounter numerous opportunities to confront racism. They cannot and should not allow their fears or unwarranted confidence to prevent them from doing the right thing. That means they should get involved, confront racism in themselves and others, and seek to make mental health delivery service more equitable. They must understand that racism involves behaviors they do *not* do, as well as behaviors they do. As Thouless (1974) explains, "So important is action that we can reasonably condemn as crooked thinking any device in thought which has as its purpose the evasion of useful or necessary action" (p. 166).

Chapter Summary

In this chapter, racism was defined. Racism is characterized by five important features: many possible behaviors, systematic behavior, preferential treatment, inequitable outcomes, and nonrandom victimization. A behavioral model that categorizes racism into its various component behaviors was also presented. Of the various forms of racism, unintentional racist acts are the most insidious. These behaviors usually go unnoticed, but their harmful consequences are far reaching.

In the following chapters, unintentional racism in counseling will be more closely examined. The scope of the discussion will be limited to individual as opposed to institutional practices. This is a problem shared by many counselors, regardless of their racial backgrounds, therapeutic orientations, or years of professional experience. The discussion will illustrate how racism exists in numerous counselor behaviors, bringing harm to minority clients. The most incredible part is that counselors, in many ways, are socialized and trained to behave as racists without even knowing it.

Notes

1. The exclusively behavioral definition of racism used in this book deviates somewhat from other usages of the term. More often than not, racism is used to identify the presumption that apparent differences between minorities and Whites can be explained biogenetically. For other points of view, see Fairchild (1991), Jones (1972), Katz and Taylor (1988), and Miles (1989, 1993).

Classification of groups of people into races is often based upon phenotypes or observed physical characteristics. From this perspective, race is a sociological phenomenon, consisting of a set of beliefs about people together with its behavior consequences. Some professionals prefer the phrase, "visible racial, ethnic group" (VREG) to designate any group of non-White people in this country (Cook & Helms, 1988). In this book, the term *race* takes on a social definition (Jones, 1992; vanden Berghe, 1967). This application recognizes the power of phenotypes to provoke attitudinal and behavioral responses. John Griffin's (1961) classic book, *Black Like Me,* graphically illustrates the force of perceived physical characteristics and their sociological consequences. Although taking a sociological stance, I acknowledge that the concept of race is questionable. Even biological-evolutionary explanations of race are dubious. For excellent discussions of the topic, refer to Montagu (1964), Yee, Fairchild, Weizman, and Wyatt (1993), and Zuckerman (1990).

Many groups such as women, gays, and handicapped persons experience systematic oppression and victimization. The behavioral definition and model of racism is helpful in understanding the mistreatment of members of these groups. However, scholarly integrity demands separate social science analyses to ferret out the special dynamics of victimization for each oppressed group.

2. According to Katz and Kahn (1978), the open system approach was developed to deal with the inadequacies of closed system thinking. The most important misconception in the closed system approach is the failure to recognize fully that organizations are dependent on inputs from their environments. In this respect, no system is ever closed or self-contained. Ridley and Mendoza (1993) call it an illusion for organizations to pay homage to open system theory without respecting their interdependence with the surrounding suprasystem.

3. Dr. John M. Taborn is credited with introducing me to the behavioral model of racism used in this book.

4

Models of Mental Health

Everyone has a yardstick of one sort or another to size up other people. Yardsticks are used, sometimes unknowingly, to gauge human behavior and determine its appropriateness. When people measure up to society's cultural values, they are labeled normal. When they do not measure up to society's cultural values, they are labeled abnormal or deviant. Behind the use of every yardstick and the labeling that goes along with it is a more basic purpose: to determine if people should change and how much they should change.

In the counseling profession, the yardsticks used to measure behavior are called models of mental health. They provide professional standards by which counselors judge normalcy and deviance. Nietzel, Bernstein, & Milich (1994) state that models help counselors (a) organize their thinking about behavior, (b) guide their clinical decisions and interventions, and (c) communicate in a common, systematic language with colleagues. Models of mental health, in effect, are tools of the counseling trade.

In this chapter, four prominent models of mental health are described: the deficit, medical, conformity, and biopsychosocial models. Despite the benefits of models as suggested by Nietzel et al. (1994), professional counselors must recognize that each has inherent limitations or the potential to be misused by counselors. Examining how counselors, many of whom are unaware of these pitfalls, perpetuate racism is of special interest.

The Deficit Model

The deficit model, as implied by its name, views ethnic minorities as flawed. This model of mental health is based on the premise that minorities have predetermined deficiencies. Thomas and Sillen (1972) observe that these assumed deficiencies were used historically to relegate minorities to an inferior status. These alleged deficiencies have often been used to explain psychopathology among minorities. There are two major variations of the deficit model.

The first variation is the genetic deficit hypothesis. It rests on the assumption that racial/ethnic minorities are deficient in desirable genes, and differences between minorities and Whites reflect their biological/genetic capacities (Atkinson, Morten, & Sue, 1993). The genetic deficit hypothesis has a long history in the social sciences. Early support can be found in the writings of Darwin (1959), deGobineau (1915), Galton (1869), Hall (1904), and Terman (1916), all of whom were prominent scholars.

The genetic deficit hypothesis can be subdivided into two categories. The intellectual deficit hypothesis claims that genetic makeup plays the predominant role in the determination of intelligence. Ethnic minorities are said to be born with inferior brains, and therefore, they have limited capacity for mental development compared to Whites (Stanton, 1960). Contemporary proponents of this view include such individuals as Hernstein (1971), Jensen (1969), Rushton (1988), Shockley (1971) and Shuey (1966), each espousing a particular rendition of this theme. The personality deficit hypothesis describes ethnic minorities as abnormal in character and behavior. This theory is sometimes also used to explain criminal behavior of minorities.

The second variation is the cultural deficit hypothesis. This variation can be similarly divided into two categories. The cultural deprivation hypothesis states that ethnic minorities have an inferior culture or no culture at all. This theory shifts the blame to the lifestyles of ethnic minorities. The cultural stress hypothesis portrays minorities as "wounded soldiers." This theory holds that minorities have broken down and become debilitated under the weight of oppression. A by-product is the inability of minorities to compete effectively in society with their White counterparts.

Unintentional Racist Implications

The deficit model is the most explicitly racist model of mental health. Most people would assume that professionals holding this viewpoint are intentional racists. The perception is especially true of professionals who hold to the genetic deficit hypothesis. Upon closer examination, however, it becomes clear that professionals who embrace the deficit model can also practice unintentional racism. This possibility exists especially for professionals who embrace the cultural deficit hypothesis. Atkinson et al. (1993) comment on this possibility:

> Ironically, it was well-intentioned white social scientists who were attempting to reject the genetically deficient model who talked about "cultural deprivation." Unfortunately, these social scientists were as much prisoners of their own cultural conditioning as those of an earlier decade. . . . The cultural deficit notion does not make sense because everyone inherits a culture. What proponents of this view were really saying was that racial/ethnic minorities do not possess "the right culture." (p. 353)

Counselors who take a cultural deficit stance tend to make one of two treatment errors. They either lower their expectations or set unrealistically high expectations of minority clients. I have had both types of expectations placed on me. When I was an inner-city high school student in Philadelphia, my guidance counselor advised me to attend the city community college. Despite my strong academic record and desire to attend a more competitive university in another state, she persisted in her advice. She would probably be surprised to learn that I now hold a Ph.D. from a prominent university. When I defended my doctoral dissertation, I encountered another type of expectation. Several members of my committee asked extremely difficult questions. My chairman later told me that my oral examination was one of the most rigorous he had ever witnessed. He believed that the line of questioning was reasonable. A well-known member of the committee, who seemed embarrassed when I saw him later, told me that I really earned my degree.

Unrealistic expectations set minority clients up for failure. Expectations set too low can lead to a self-fulfilling prophecy. Expectations set too high may be impossible to achieve. Although some minority clients are assertive enough to challenge these expectations, many are not. What makes these expectations most damaging is that the experience of failure in counseling may reinforce preexisting feelings of inadequacy. The deficit model, even in its less blatantly racist variations, is unsuited for empowering minority clients.

The Medical Model

The medical model is the dominant framework used by mental health professionals to understand and treat psychological problems. The model is based on an assumed analogy between psychological disorders and physical problems (Turner & Cumming, 1967). Classical psychoanalysis, a major impetus behind the medical model, is unsurpassed in shaping the thinking and practice of mental health treatment. Sigmund Freud, the founder of psychoanalysis, was a Vienna neurologist. His medical orientation naturally influenced the development of his clinical theory and practice. Many modern day professionals and a large segment of the general population continue to accept the medical model. The model has several key features.

First, the focus is on illness. Psychological problems are viewed as diseases just like physical diseases. Hersch (1968) notes that the terms *illness* and *disease* have been defined as the presence of symptoms. On this topic, Phares (1992) states: "Nowhere is this view better illustrated than by statements such as 'This patient is *suffering* from schizophrenia' or 'This patient has been *afflicted* by these phobias for many years' " (p. 133). By implication, mental health is a condition based on the absence of symptoms. Successful intervention in mental illness involves first diagnosing and than destroying the underlying disease.

Second, the classical doctor-patient relationship is emphasized. Counseling professionals are regarded as experts and knowledgeable authorities. They are expected to be highly trained, skilled, and almost omnipotent. Clients, on the other hand, are regarded as needy recipients of the counselor's services. They are expected to accept the counselor's diagnosis and comply unquestioningly with the treatment recommendations.

Third, the time requirements of treatment are long-term. Clients may be expected to spend months or even years in therapy, because the real work of change is in-depth. Short-term therapy is regarded as superficial, ineffective, and a quick fix. This is because deeper conflicts of the client, which build up over years, are not adequately treated.

Finally, the approach to treatment involves a verbal endeavor. Beginning with Freud's notions of catharsis and free association, individual insight-oriented psychotherapy has been the prevailing mode of mental health treatment. In fact, it has been called a "talking cure." Therapists ask provoking questions to get patients to self-disclose. Therapists also interpret their patients' disclosures. For therapy to be successful, patients must be highly verbal and capable of discussing their intimate thoughts and feelings.

Unintentional Racist Implications

To determine exactly how the use of the medical model results in unintentional racism, a brief review of Freud's theory of personality is needed. The theory divides personality structure into three antagonistic systems: the id, superego, and ego.

The *id* is the primitive, unconscious part of personality. It is the storehouse of libido, the person's psychic energy. The id constantly attempts to avoid pain and gain pleasure by discharging unrestrained sexual and aggressive impulses. Freud called this the pleasure principle.

The *superego* represents the person's moral attitudes and corresponds to one's conscience. This system learns its ideas of right and wrong from family and society. The superego attempts to ward off the pleasure-seeking impulses of the id. In addition, it attempts to guard its uncompromising moral values.

The *ego* stands between the id and superego. It has two roles. Like a referee in a sports event, the ego mediates the conflicting demands of the other two systems. Freud called this the synthetic function. The ego also guides the person to meet the demands of the real world. Freud called this the executive function.

All three components of personality get their energy from the id instincts, and everyone has a limited supply of energy. The more energy the ego uses to perform its synthetic function, the less it has to perform its executive function. According to Freud, the synthetic role of the ego takes precedent over the executive role. If valuable energy is expended or overused in performing synthetic activity, energy is no longer available for relating to the outside world. Freud (1949) states that the internal claims of the id and superego weaken the ego's ties to external reality. When this happens, the person suffers from neurosis: a condition of an ego weakened by internal conflict and forced to adopt inappropriate coping strategies. Freud likens the conflict to a civil war. Ruch (1967) elaborates on this struggle:

> Caught in this conflict, the ego usually resorts to some form of compromise which will at least partially satisfy both libido and conscience. Inability of the ego to make such a compromise leads to the appearance of neurotic symptoms. (p. 120)

Freud's method of therapy follows his concept of neurosis. Because the patient's problems are rooted in the unconscious, the goals of analysis are to: (a) uncover repressed conflicts, (b) raise them to the level of preconscious, and (c) return the ego to controlling the id's drives and relating effectively to reality. To achieve these goals, the analyst must overcome the patient's strategies of repressing material in the unconscious. Initially, the analyst takes over the role of the patient's superego, which scrutinizes all psychological material. Then the therapist interprets the material that is brought to consciousness by free association or analysis of slips of the tongue and dreams. The therapist also traces the material back to its origins in the patient's childhood.

The implications of the medical model for unintentional racism in counseling are as follows.

1. *Tendency to Overpathologize.* The persistent focus on illness allows external explanations of behavior to be overlooked. Reiff (1967) points out that professionals find it easy to associate disturbance with everyone and difficult to associate health or normalcy with anyone. As victims of racism, ethnic minorities are more likely than other clients to be blamed for their problems and given a pathological label. Professionals who are committed to the medical model tend to search for intrapsychic explanations of disturbing symptoms. When treating minority clients, they often overlook the possibility that puzzling behavior is a reflection of social pathologies such as racism, discrimination, poverty, inadequate health care, and poor education. Such a superficial inspection is much like signaling out an "acting out" identified patient as the primary source of the problem in a dysfunctional family system.

2. *Limited Social Applicability.* The pervasive influence of Freudian psychology gave rise to the psychiatric worldview (Kuriloff, 1970). According to Riessman and Miller (1964), society tends to evaluate all social problems, from political to educational, in intrapsychic, psychoanalytic terms. To some extent, the model is helpful in conceptualizing individual problems. However, the psychiatric worldview is inadequate for conceptualizing racism and other social pathologies. Eisenberg (1962) states:

> Society is more than an aggregate of its individual members. When systems in the social organism go awry, it is absurd to attempt their correction by medicating the individuals whose aberrations are secondary or tertiary order consequences of the basic lesions. (p. 789)

The medical model has an indirect effect on minority mental health. It is not helpful in analyzing and remediating the social conditions that give rise to much of the distress among minorities. Actually, it does the opposite. By proffering causal rather than consequential explanations of racism, the medical model perpetuates the problem it seeks to overcome. When social reformers attack racism and other forms of oppression, they emphasize attitude change, often leaving insidious racist behaviors unchallenged.

3. *Inaccessibility of Services to Minorities.* Because the goal of treatment is in-depth change, traditional psychotherapy tends to be long-term. The expense and time involved in this form of therapy eliminates a large pool of potential patients, especially minorities who are poor. Kuriloff (1970) points out that even among those clients who are served, the treatment is of limited value. He further notes that public agencies servicing these consumers "always employ it in a 'watered down' version. Professionals, unable to go either as 'deep' or as long as the treatment model prescribes, must compromise and seek short cuts which are, by definition, inferior techniques" (p. 19).

4. *Failure to Teach Coping Skills.* Preoccupation with synthetic ego functions to the exclusion of executive functions tends to obfuscate how minorities otherwise manage and cope with reality. Even among minority clients who successfully resolve intrapsychic conflicts, the model does not help them take the next step: learning to negotiate the stressful demands of reality. For many minorities, their difficulties result from executive ego deficiencies rather than intrapsychic conflict (Kuriloff, 1970). For example, minority clients may not have good job search or interviewing skills, although they are perfectly capable of maintaining gainful employment. The problem-analysis approach of the medical model is inadequate for meeting the problem-solving needs of many minorities.

5. *Role Confusion of Therapeutic Participants.* The implicit expert role of the therapist and passive role of the client create a paradox in multicultural counseling. In fact, this situation contradicts some of the real requirements for change. On the one hand, many counselors do not understand the background or culture of minority clients. They often use counseling sessions to acquire cultural expertise. On the other hand, minority clients are the ones expected to educate counselors about their culture. When these clients are asked to enlighten the counselor, counseling may not be of much benefit to them. Paradoxically, the so-called expert is unable to translate the cultural information into therapeutic action (Ridley, Mendoza, Kanitz, Angermeier, & Zenk, 1994).

The Conformity Model

The conformity model (or sociocultural model) has evolved out of the scientific tradition of the social sciences. It assumes the normal distribution of characteristics and behaviors throughout a population. Social scientists claim that many personality variables can be shown to be normally distributed, once enough observations of those variables are made. The *normal curve* is a powerful statistical concept used to plot a frequency distribution. It is bell-shaped and symmetrical (refer to Figure 4.1).

Interpretation of individual behavior is referenced to the normative or standardization sample of the population. The normative sample is a group of representative members of the population. Theoretically, this group provides a set of *norms* against which individual behavior is compared. Norms provide an external standard, permitting interpretation of individual behavior as "good," "average," or "poor." High-frequency behavior in a population is judged as healthy or normal. Low-frequency behavior, on the other hand, is judged as deviant or abnormal. Wallace (1970) uses the concept *modal personality* to denote "any method that characterizes the personality typical of a culturally bounded population by the central tendency of a defined frequency distribution" (p. 152).

Two versions of the sociocultural model exist: the etic and emic.

Etic. Etic is a culturally universal or generalized model of mental health. It defines behavior patterns on a fixed adjustment/maladjustment continuum (Ridley, 1986a). The model promotes a standard of normalcy that spans cultural, ethnic, and racial lines. The criteria for interpreting behavior always remain constant, regardless of the cultural context or persons being judged. Using this yardstick, persons in the South Bronx, Peking, Papua, New Guinea, and Cairo, Egypt, would all be judged against the same norms. Their respective backgrounds would not be taken into consideration.

Emic. Emic is a culturally sensitive or specific model of mental health. Draguns (1989) suggests that norms and expectations vary across cultures. This model construes mental health in terms of divergent attitudes, values, and behaviors that arise out of specific cultures. Similar overt behaviors may mean something different to people of different backgrounds. On the other hand, different behaviors could have similar meanings across various cultures. This implies that the valid interpretation of behavior rests upon a person's indigenous cultural norms. Chess, Clark, and Thomas (1953)

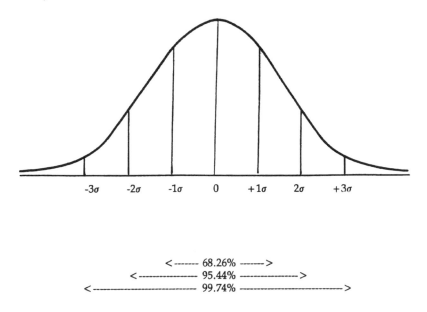

Figure 4.1. Bell-Shaped Curve

state that behavior interpreted as pathological in one culture may be interpreted as healthy adaptation in another.

Unintentional Racist Implications

The major racist implication of the conformity model is the imposition of majority group values on minority clients. Phares (1992) describes several relevant problems associated with the conformity model: (a) cutoff points (i.e., How deviant must a person be to acquire the magic designation of deviant?); (b) number of deviations (i.e., How often must a person nonconform or show deviations from the norm to be considered deviant?); and (c) acute versus chronic behaviors (i.e., To what extent is maladjustment contingent upon the acuteness or chronicity of behavior?).

Many counselors do not struggle with these questions, let alone realize the implications of leaving them unanswered. In theory, they may acknowledge emic and etic distinctions. In practice, they often adopt a "pseudoetic approach" (Triandis, Malpass, & Davidson, 1973). They generalize their own etic values and techniques across cultures. In so doing, they violate the principle of norm-referenced interpretation: An individual can only be compared with a group of people who have matching characteristics and are randomly selected representatives of the target population. Belkin (1984) states, "Unintentionally and through ignorance counselors frequently impose their own cultural values upon minority clients" (p. 536).

Clinical cases illustrating the problems associated with overlooking cultural influences on behavior abound in the literature (e.g., Lum, 1992; Martinez, 1988; Pinderhughes, 1989; Ramos-McKay, Comas-Díaz, & Rivera, 1988; Thompson, Blueye, Smith, & Walker, 1983). The discussion by Thompson and colleagues (1983) of a patient labeled a "crazy Indian" is a clinical case in point. The emergency room physician, who made the initial diagnosis, failed to take into account the cultural and circumstantial dimensions of the presenting problem. Likewise, the nurse saw the patient as impulsive and potentially violent. An Indian psychiatric resident was called in to see the patient. After interviewing the patient, the psychiatrist formed a different impression:

> In making my psychiatric assessment of this man's situation it was clear that I was not being asked to deal with "pure" psychopathology. . . . I knew that if this man had been seen by a doctor with no training in cultural psychiatry he might well have been diagnosed as psychotic and/or alcoholic, deemed dangerous to himself and others, and committed to a psychiatric ward. (Thompson et al., 1983, p. 271)

The Biopsychosocial Model

The biopsychosocial model is a relatively recent innovation, although its historical roots run deep. The early Greek philosophers, for example, first paid attention to the mind-body relationship. The model emphasizes the whole person. Unlike the almost exclusive intrapsychic focus of the medical model, the biopsychosocial model attempts to understand people by examining every major influence upon human functioning. The model considers physical health, interpersonal and social competence, and psychological and emotional well-being (Lewis, Sperry, & Carlson, 1993). Taylor (1990) gives this definition of the biopsychosocial model:

> Research in behavioral medicine and, correspondingly, in health psychology has taken the position that biological, psychological, and social factors are implicated in all stages of health and illness, ranging from those behaviors and states that keep people healthy to those that produce severe, long-term, and debilitating disease. (p. 40)

According to Engel (1977), the model is based upon systems thinking. When applied to psychological intervention, Sperry (1988) calls the model biopsychosocial therapy. With this view in mind, a major emphasis in treatment is changing behavior to prevent or mitigate disease. As such, it is a health promotion model. Matarazzo (1980) argues that psychology has an increasing role in the promotion and maintenance of health, prevention and treatment of illness, and identification of factors involved in health and illness.

Krantz, Grunberg, and Baum (1985) describe three processes by which behavior influences health and disease. These processes offer insight into understanding people biopsychosocially, and they are targets of intervention. These include:

- **Effects of stress on health.** Chronic stress ultimately produces tissue changes, even when people do not engage in direct harmful behaviors.
- **Harmful behaviors and lifestyles.** Some behaviors cause illness. Among the more prominent are cigarette smoking, poor diets, lack of exercise, excessive alcohol consumption, drug abuse, and poor hygienic practices. Some harmful behaviors reflect cultural practices, and others are idiosyncratic.
- **Reaction to illness.** Some people respond inappropriately to illness. They may deny the significance or severity of their symptoms, delay getting medical attention, or fail to comply with treatment or rehabilitation programs.

Unintentional Racist Implications

The biopsychosocial model is not inherently racist. Because the model involves a comprehensive approach to understanding health and illness, it does not have a bias that could lead to misinterpretation of behavior. In that sense, it stands apart from the other models of mental health. When the biopsychosocial model is used appropriately, it is an effective tool for treating minority clients. Counselors using the model should be able to gather and integrate a broad range of information relevant to their clients' presenting problems. Racism may occur when the model is misused or not used at all. There are two important implications for the misuse or nonuse of the biopsychosocial model.

1. *Failure to Treat Clients Holistically.* An imminent danger in treating minorities lies in disregarding all of the major influences upon them. A major criticism in the literature has been the tendency to overlook social factors such as racism and oppression and other stressors. Psychology has been identified as the "handmaiden of the status quo" (Halleck, 1971,

p. 30). Given the influential role of poverty, dietary deficiencies, poor access to medical treatment, lower quality education, and other social factors, it is easy to see how counselors who do not use the biopsychosocial model unintentionally mistreat minority clients. They miss many opportunities to include these factors in the formula for assessment and treatment planning. The problem is compounded by the fact that many counselors were trained before the biopsychosocial model became a valued tool of the profession. In many training and practice contexts, the model remains an underutilized tool.

2. *Failure to Promote Health.* Most mental health services to minorities are rehabilitative. These services attempt to reduce the residual effects and adverse consequences of severe disturbance. Limited attention is given to illness prevention and health promotion, even though epidemiological studies report higher rates of major diseases in minority communities. For example, a disproportionate number of HIV-infected cases are represented among African Americans and Latinos (Centers for Disease Control, 1992). Unintentional racism is probably perpetuated by counselors who do not emphasize prevention or teach minority clients health behaviors. The problem is compounded by the general failure of the mental health profession to design outreach programs that seek to minimize stress, harmful behaviors and lifestyles, and inappropriate reactions to illness in minority communities. Primary mental health prevention is conspicuously unavailable to many minorities.

Chapter Summary

Four prominent models of mental health were described: the deficit, medical, conformity, and biopsychosocial models. As yardsticks for measuring normalcy and abnormalcy, they are powerful tools used by mental health professionals. This chapter described how the use, misuse, or lack of use of these models perpetuates unintentional racism. Counselors often do not appropriately adapt these models to minority clients. The most insidious problems probably occur when counselors use the medical model indiscriminately and do not make use of the biopsychosocial model.

5

Judgmental and Inferential Errors

Clinical decision making is an integral part of counseling. The judgment of counselors may be second in importance only to the counseling relationship. Dumont and Lecomte (1987) define counseling and psychotherapy as an inferential process whereby counselors engage in clinical reasoning and make causal inferences on the basis of information imparted to them. Counselors are assumed to be skilled in logical reasoning and inference making, suggesting that their judgments are objective and impartial.

This chapter explores clinical decision making. The process is complex and challenging, and counselors are subject to numerous judgmental and inferential errors. Decision making is further complicated by the nuances of meaning arising out of racial and cultural differences. Westermeyer (1987) reports that misdiagnosis, overestimation, underestimation, or neglect of psychopathology are frequent problems when clinicans and patients have different cultural backgrounds. The variety of judgmental errors counselors make regarding minority clients is the focus of this chapter.

Why Is Decision Making Difficult?

Several factors make clinical decision making difficult. People are complex. They are a unique mixture of many emotions, life experiences, values, attitudes, personal preferences, coping styles, and psychological issues. When clients show up for counseling, they exhibit these complex features (Dumont & Lecomte, 1987). Then counselors have to sift through this complexity in an effort to figure out each client.

Beside being complex, many clients do not describe themselves or their experiences completely and coherently. Instead, their self-disclosures are often fragmented, incoherent, and emotionally charged. Because of their psychological pain and feelings of vulnerability, clients often omit and distort crucial information about themselves. When this happens, counselors find it extremely difficult to sort out the pieces and separate what is real from clever distortions or distractions. In addition, counselors may misread minority clients. Sue and Sue (1977, 1990) discuss at length the differences in verbal, nonverbal, paralinguistic, proxemic, kinesic, and contextual communication styles operative in multicultural counseling. They also describe how generic characteristics of counseling are culturally bound. Counselors who are inattentive to these cultural variables increase their chances of making judgmental errors.

Strohmer and Shivy (1992) describe the complexity of clinical decision making from the perspective of information processing:

> The counseling process is a massive information processing task in which the counselor is bombarded by a large volume of complex data. Cognitive psychology, as well as counseling experience tells us that, as counselors, we are realistically unable to attend to all the information available in the counseling interaction. Counselors simply cannot process the variety of both verbal and nonverbal stimuli that make up a counseling session, and therefore must learn to attend selectively to the information presented. Perhaps what distinguishes talented and professional counselors from simple interviewers is the ability to identify, attend to, and adequately process the salient information a client provides. The complex nature of this information process and decision making task must certainly test the counselor's skill, and make the counselors' ability to operate as a scientist/practitioner critically important. (p. 2)

In addition, counselors bring to counseling their own biases and hidden agendas. Like everyone, counselors are influenced by a host of factors that may impair their judgment. There is considerable literature, for example,

Table 5.1 Types of Clinical Decisions

Diagnoses
Prognoses
Referrals
Treatment planning
Selection of interventions
Frequency of treatment
Termination
Medical therapy
Reporting abuse or neglect
Duty to warn
Involuntary commitments
Deciding the importance of case history data
Interpreting test data

---

indicating that judgment is biased in the direction of preexisting stereotypes when the material to be judged is ambiguous or complex. Of course, ambiguity and complexity are just the sort of things counselors regularly face. Therefore, they need to be alert, not only to biases in judgment, but also to their personal biases as judges. Counselors' judgments may be especially clouded when they interact with clients of other races and cultures or those who have different worldviews.

The Need for Judgmental Accuracy

Despite the difficulty in clinical decision making, counselors are continually expected to use client information in forming impressions or hypotheses about them (Morrow & Deidan, 1992; Spengler, 1992). But this is not the full extent of decision making. It includes all activities in which counselors form impressions or hypotheses. Table 5.1 lists many of the types of decisions counselors make.

Decision making in counseling is inevitable. It is not a matter of whether or not counselors will make clinical decisions. It is a matter of what decisions counselors will make, how they will use client information in decision making, and how valid their decisions will be.

Obviously, counselors should make valid clinical decisions. Their decisions should be impartial, reflecting as accurate a picture of clients as possible (Dumont & Lecomte, 1987). Also, their decisions should cater to

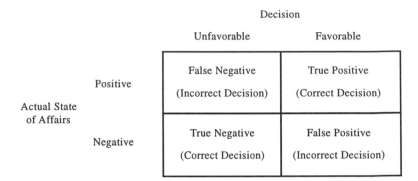

Figure 5.1. Four Categories of Decisions

the best interest of the clients. If skilled counselors could treat the same client, they ought to formulate similar clinical judgments. Their decisions should not be biased by the background of either client or counselor or the complexity and nature of the client's presenting problem(s) (Ridley, 1986b).

Accurate clinical decision making is necessary to ensure that clients receive equitable and reliable service delivery. Inaccurate decision making, by contrast, results in poor service delivery. Gambrill (1990) points out some of the adverse consequences of clinicians making bad decisions:

> Errors in judgment may result in misattributing client problems to internal mental disorders; overlooking pathology; selecting weak or ineffective intervention methods; or predicting incorrectly suicidal potential, need for hospitalization, or future recurrence of violent acts. (p. 3)

Four Types of Decisions

The many decisions made by counselors generally fall into four categories: true positives, false positives, false negatives, and true negatives. Two of these types of decisions are correct, and two are incorrect. See Figure 5.1.

1. True Positive

A true positive is a favorable decision or judgment that is correct. Smirnow and Bruhn (1984) give an excellent case study involving sound diagnosis and treatment planning. Juan is a 7-year-old boy of very poor, rural Hispanic immigrant parents. He was seen in a community mental health center and successfully treated for encopresis, an eating disorder and school phobia. The success of therapy, which lasted 21 sessions over an 8-month period, hinged on the ability of the therapist to "distinguish pathology from subcultural beliefs and practices" (p. 24). This enabled the therapist to select appropriate interventions. It is important to acknowledge that some clinicians do make good clinical decisions about minority clients.

2. False Positive

A false positive is a favorable decision that is incorrect. Westermeyer (1987) describes the case of a 14-year-old Cambodian boy. He was referred to the school counselor because of his disruptive classroom behavior. No psychological assessment had been undertaken prior to his placement, even though he had been withdrawn from school in Asia. There he had difficulty learning, and during his early childhood, he had a prolonged fever with a coma. When a physical examination was given, he showed "soft signs" of brain damage. Intellectual testing revealed mild mental retardation. When placed in a school program for children with mental retardation, he did well. The original decision to place him in a regular classroom was a false positive. It assumed a higher level of functioning than was true of him.

3. False Negative

A false negative is an unfavorable decision that is incorrect. Westermeyer (1987) describes a 48-year-old Chinese woman. She was placed on a regimen of antipsychotic and antidepressant medication. Then she lost weight and hope and became more immobilized. At the time of her diagnosis, she expressed a belief that her deceased mother, who appeared in her dreams, was attempting to induce the patient's own death and bring her to the next world. Clinicians later reinterpreted this symptom as a culturally consistent belief instead of a delusion. There is a common harbinger of death in the dreams of some Asian patients. The patient responded well to the discontinuation of antipsychotic medication, reduction in dosage of antidepressant medication, and reinstitution of weekly psychotherapy.

4. True Negative

A true negative is a negative decision that is correct. A clinical psychologist judged a Japanese American client to have suicidal potential and accordingly obtained involuntary commitment. The patient somehow escaped from the psychiatric hospital and made an unsuccessful suicide attempt. The judgment of the psychologist about the client was negative but accurate.

Prevalent Judgmental Errors

Counselors are constantly confronted with decisions such as those just described. Competent counselors attempt to maximize correct decision making and minimize incorrect decision making. They attempt to make as many true positive and true negative decisions while making as few false positive and false negative decisions as possible. This section describes prevalent errors that counselors make in regard to minority clients.

Fundamental Attribution Error

Counselors tend to overestimate the importance of personality or dispositional factors and overlook situational variables in understanding client problems (Batson, Jones, & Cochran, 1979; Dumont & Lecomte, 1987; Wills, 1978). This error is very common. Counselors readily attribute client problems to broad personal dispositions, expecting consistency of client behavior across dissimilar situations. They see client behaviors as freely selected, and they fail to consider situational coercions that lead to particular behaviors (Ross, 1977).

Goffman (1961) observes fundamental attribution bias in a clinical setting:

> I have seen a therapist deal with a Negro patient's complaints about race relations in a partially segregated hospital by telling the patient that he must ask himself why he, among all the other Negroes present, chose this particular moment to express this feeling, and what this expression could mean about him as a person, apart from the state of race relations in the hospital at the time. (pp. 376-377)

In this case, the patient's problems were attributed to personal or dispositional traits. The context in which the so-called problems occurred—a partially segregated hospital—was completely ignored by the therapist. More than likely, the victim-blaming of this patient resulted in unwarranted labeling.

Diagnostic Overshadowing

Another type of judgmental error is diagnostic overshadowing. This is the tendency of counselors to use one diagnosis to obscure or minimize the importance of another diagnosis. In such cases, counselors underdiagnose psychopathology and minimize the client's need for treatment. They disregard certain types of assessment information in favor of others. Counselors have been shown to overshadow vocational problems with personal problems (Spengler, Blustein, & Strohmer, 1990) and psychopathology with intellectual functioning problems (Reiss & Szyszko, 1983).

Case Example. A Native American student went to the student counseling center on a university campus. She was a sophomore and needed to select a major field of study. Although she was not completely adjusted to life off the reservation, she had made friends with a small group of Indian students. Most of her friends were majoring in Native American studies, but she was interested in science. When she went to counseling, the counselor was intrigued by her Indianness and her struggle to adjust in a predominantly White university. The counselor preferred to work with the client on personal problems, overshadowing her pressing need to select a major. An unbiased counselor would pay more attention to the client's quandary. Among the possible concerns of the client could be (a) a feeling of guilt for not pursuing a major in Native American studies, (b) uncertainty that she could be successful in a science field, and (c) indecision about whether to major in chemistry or biology.

Confirmatory Bias

Confirmatory bias is the tendency of counselors to confirm their assumptions or initial hypotheses. Counselors who show confirmatory bias "find" evidence to support their suppositions, even when there is more contrary evidence (Strohmer & Shivy, 1992). Meehl (1960) observes that clinicians form "images" of their clients within the first 4 hours of treatment. Then they staunchly adhere to their beliefs, expectations, and hypotheses about clients. Rosenhan (1973) finds that clinicians usually expect to observe pathology and report it even when there is little evidence on which to base their conclusions.

Case Example. David Lee, a Chinese American, was a successful architectural engineer. During the past 2 months, he had experienced intense headaches and lower back pain. He went to his family physician who gave him a thorough examination. However, the physician could not find any physical problems. The physician referred David to a psychiatrist. The psychiatrist remembered reading that Asians do not like to discuss personal problems because this brings shame upon their families. Then the psychiatrist concluded that David was somaticizing and repressing his feelings. In the meantime, the psychiatrist dismissed the almost obvious fact that David's success as an entrepreneur was catching up with him. David started a consulting business 7 months ago. He works 12 to 14 hours a day. Recently, he won several impressive contracts. In addition, his wife has a busy career, and they literally scramble to take care of domestic responsibilities. David Lee was actually in a state of distress.

Judgmental Heuristics

Counselors often use quick decision rules known as judgmental heuristics. These rules short circuit the decision-making process. Counselors use these decision rules almost automatically, without thinking through the nature of their decisions. Making snap decisions prevents counselors from behaving as true scientist-practitioners, who by definition gather as much information as possible in formulating a clinical hypothesis.

There are two kinds of judgmental heuristics: availability heuristics and anchoring heuristics. Availability heuristics base judgments on information saliency. Counselors use relevant information that easily comes to memory. At the same time, they do not search for less salient, less consistent information.

Anchoring heuristics base judgments on the chronology of information. Counselors hold on to initial information, downplaying or ignoring the importance of information acquired later. Strohmer and Shivy (1992) state that counselors may anchor to salient client information early during an assessment. As a result, they often disregard contradictory information, which could be found if counselors were skillful in searching for it.

Case Example. A 35-year-old African American named Henry was seen at the Outpatient Clinic of the Veterans Administration Hospital in Chicago. He had recently lost his job and appeared highly agitated. The clinical psychologist administered the MMPI. The profile indicated an elevation on Scale 6, suggesting sensitivity, guardedness, and suspiciousness. The psychologist diagnosed the client as paranoid. A more thorough investigation into the client's experience could contradict the psychologist's judgment. Elevated scores on Scale 6 of the MMPI are more common among African American males. Moreover, Henry worked in a factory filled with subtle racial tension. When several White employees tried to set him up, he physically assaulted one of them. Management fired him because he was "hostile and aggressive," and there was no tangible proof anyone was bothering him. The diagnosis of paranoia ignored Henry's experience as an African American male who must deal with the reality of racism.

Reconstructive Memory

Sometimes people fill gaps in their memory or alter their memories to be consistent with their present experience (Loftus & Loftus, 1980; Snyder & Uranowitz, 1978; Wells, 1982). This cognitive process was first postulated by Bartlett (1932). It is likely to occur when there is a need to create important categories such as a diagnosis. Wells (1982) reports that people who reconstruct memory are less likely to remember specific information with accuracy. He also suggests that people tend to be confident in the accuracy of their memory, although they are under the illusion that the reconstruction is a recall of factual information.

Morrow and Deidan (1992) describe why documentation helps to avoid reconstructive memory:

> Case notes are vital because they are "the only record or documentation of what transpires between a counselor and a client." . . . Despite the significance of accurate records, we were unable to find any investigations of reconstructive memory in counseling. (p. 575)

Besides the clinical value of accurate record keeping, Keith-Spiegel and Koocher (1985) remind counselors of its ethical importance. Reconstructive memory can jeopardize the welfare of minority consumers.

Case Example. Phillip Greenwood is a psychology intern at a comprehensive community mental health center in Houston. The center serves a large Hispanic and Black clientele. Due to the severe economic recession and considerable job layoffs, the census at the center is high. During the past couple of weeks, Phillip had put off writing case notes until the end of the week. Although Phillip is extremely bright and has a good memory, he inadvertently wrote incorrect information in several case summaries. In one case, he wrote that a Hispanic female was a victim of assault. In actuality, the woman told him that she feared being assaulted because of the recent wave of crime and violence in her community. Phillip also wrote that she should consider joining a victims survivors group.

Overconfidence

Some clinicians are overconfident in their clinical judgment (Arkes, 1981; Lichtenstein, Fischhoff, & Phillips, 1982). Holsopple and Phelan (1954) found a negative relationship between clinicians' confidence and their diagnostic accuracy. The most confident clinicians tend to be the least accurate.

Numerous factors, no doubt, contribute to overconfidence. Einhorn and Hogarth (1978) note that treatment effects are one factor. If a client improves for any reason, the therapist may attribute the improvement to the treatment. In certain situations, improvement may be due to a placebo, not the efficacy of an intervention. Koriat, Lichtenstein, and Fischhoff (1980) suggest another reason for unwarranted confidence. People can generate support for their decisions easier than they can generate contradictory evidence.

Case Example. Rafic Ali is a 29-year-old Arab from Iraq. He has gotten into several heated conflicts with a neighbor. Both parties have legitimate gripes, although most of the problems arise out of cultural misunderstanding. Rafic was so upset that he went to see a therapist in private practice. Although Rafic is sympathetic to Arab causes, he is basically a peaceloving person. In fact, he has hesitated to return home since completing his M.B.A. at an American university. He is not sure if he wants to live with unrest, Arab militancy, and the reign of Saddam Hussein. Unfortunately, the therapist saw Rafic as another radical Arab. He saw the conflict with the neighbor as Rafic's animosity toward Americans. The recent bombing and terrorism in New York City added weight to the therapist's confidence in his opinion of the client.

A Prevalent Judgmental Error: The Attribution of Paranoia

Most forms of counseling encourage client growth through self-disclosure. This emphasis has its roots in the Freudian notion of free association and catharsis. One of the roles of counselors is to help clients explore and understand their feelings and behaviors. Presumably, clients gain insight into themselves as they self-disclose and get feedback from their counselors.

Several authors describe the reluctance of minority clients to disclose themselves in therapy, especially to White counselors (e.g., Ridley, 1984; 1986; Sue & Sue, 1990; Thompson, Worthington, & Atkinson, 1994). Many minorities have been conditioned to be cautious and mistrusting of White counselors. Harrison (1975) pinpoints this problem in his comments on the Black client:

> White society's traditional expectations of blacks have generated role behaviors that often contribute to a certain lack of openness, "gaming," and "telling the man what he would like to hear." Previous negative experiences with whites may cause blacks to develop both sensitivity and concealment of true feeling. Self-disclosure, which is basic to the counseling process, has been found to be greater among whites than blacks. . . . The hesitance of blacks to fully disclose themselves, often viewed as "playing it cool," suggests a cautiousness and initial lack of trust in the person to whom one is to disclose. Under such circumstances, establishing rapport with the counselee is more difficult, requiring sensitive and skillful counselor intervention in order to facilitate authentic communication. (p. 132)

By expecting minorities to disclose themselves, White counselors inadvertently create a paradoxical situation. On the one hand, minority clients may protect themselves by remaining tight-mouthed about their problems. In so doing, they forfeit the potential benefits of counseling. On the other hand, minority clients may choose to open themselves. In so doing, they risk being misunderstood by their counselors. Thus minority clients sometimes find themselves in a no-win situation (Ridley & Tan, 1986).

Ridley (1984) describes two dimensions of interpersonal functioning related to self-disclosure. The discussion is aimed at Black clients. However, the dynamics apply to clients of other minority groups. *Cultural paranoia* is a healthy reaction to racism. The minority client who fears the White counselor and avoids self-disclosure fits this category. *Functional paranoia* is an unhealthy psychological condition. Minority clients who have a pervasive suspicion fit this category. They would not disclose to any counselor regardless of race. A four-mode typology that categorizes minority clients according to these two dimensions is presented in Figure 5.2.

In Mode 1, the intercultural nonparanoiac discloser is a client who is low on both functional and cultural paranoia. This client typically self-discloses to counselors of any race. This acknowledges the fact that some

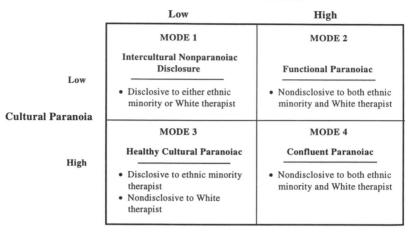

Figure 5.2. Typology of Ethnic Minority Client Self-Disclosure

SOURCE: Ridley, C. R. (1989). Racism in counseling as an adversive behavioral process. In P. B. Pedersen, J. G. Draguns, W. J. Lonner, & J. E. Trimble (Eds.). *Counseling across cultures* (3rd ed.) (pp. 55-77). Honolulu: University of Hawaii Press. Reprinted by permission.

multicultural relationships are effective. Nevertheless, this type of client is a rarity.

In Mode 2, the functional paranoiac is a client who has a true clinical paranoid disorder. This client does not disclose to any counselors, including members of the same race. This client has unusual fears of persecution, being spied upon, or trailed.

In Mode 3, the healthy cultural paranoiac is a client who attempts to protect himself or herself from racism and discrimination. Grier and Cobbs (1968, 1992), two Black psychiatrists, first described healthy cultural paranoia. This client is typically nondisclosing to White counselors but open to counselors of his or her own race. Many minority clients seem to fall into this category.

In Mode 4, the confluent paranoiac is a client who has both a strong reaction to racism and traditional paranoid condition. This is the most difficult minority client to treat because of the complex interaction of cultural and functional paranoia. Like the functional paranoiac, this client is closed to counselors of any race.

The majority of minority clients exhibit an appropriate reaction to racism. Ironically, many Mode 3 clients are classified as Mode 2, functional paranoiacs. In this case, the diagnosis is independent of the client's actual mental health status. Misunderstanding the minority client's reluctance to self-disclose contributes significantly to the overrepresentation of minorities in pathological categories. There is evidence that the diagnosis of schizophrenia, especially of the paranoid type, is being misapplied to minorities (Kleiner, Tuckman, & Lavell, 1960; Pavkov, Lewis, & Lyons, 1989; Steinberg, Pardes, Bjork, & Sporty, 1977).

Chapter Summary

Clinical decision making is an integral part of counseling. It occurs during all phases of the counseling process and requires counselors to make many different types of decisions. Despite the need for counselors to be objective and impartial, they make numerous judgmental and inferential errors. Racial and cultural factors further complicate the decision-making process, causing multiculturally incompetent counselors to be even more ineffective as decision makers. This chapter highlighted specific errors made by counselors with particular emphasis on their misjudgments about minority clients.

6

Defensive Racial Dynamics

The counselor-client relationship is often regarded as the most important aspect of counseling. As the context of change, a good counseling relationship enables a client to self-disclose, explore intrapsychic conflicts, take risks, and work through personal problems. Gelso and Fretz (1992) suggest that the application of techniques by an expert is less important than the relationship that develops between the client and counselor. Highlen and Hill (1984) are even more zealous. They see the relationship as the *sine quo non* of counseling.

A major obstacle to developing a good counseling relationship is defensiveness. The client or counselor may behave defensively toward the other participant. Sometimes both participants are defensive, creating a sort of therapeutic gridlock. Sigmund Freud (1926/1989) originally conceptualized the idea of defense mechanisms. He believed that people use defenses to protect themselves when they feel threatened. Clark (1991) defines a defense mechanism as an "unconscious distortion of reality that reduces painful affect and conflict through automatic and habitual responses" (p. 276). His helpful definition includes four important characteristics common to all defense mechanisms.

- **Unconscious motivation.** People are unaware of their defensiveness and the motives underlying their defensive behavior. They hide parts of who they are from themselves. The hidden sources of motivation usually reside in the region of unconsciousness.

- **Distortion or denial of reality.** When people are defensive, they do not look at reality objectively—the way it really is. Typically, they paint an idealized picture of reality—the way they would like it to be. Then they relate to the world on the basis of their distortion or denial.

- **Reduction of emotional pain.** Defense mechanisms serve an important purpose. They blunt emotional pain and intrapsychic conflict. In a sense, they are bandage solutions to emotional pain.

- **Automatic and habitual responsiveness.** Defensiveness quickly triggers behavior that expresses intrapsychic conflict. The behavior occurs automatically and as a reaction to emotional pain.

Descriptions of the major defenses can be found in basic counseling textbooks (e.g., Corey, 1991; Gladding, 1992). A random survey of the literature would easily reveal many defense mechanisms. In this chapter, eight racially related defenses are discussed. These defense mechanisms are important dynamics in counseling but manage to go unacknowledged. Some of these defenses are exhibited by counselors and others by clients. Defensive counselors or counselors who mishandle a minority client's defensiveness undermine the counseling relationship (Sandler & Freud, 1985) and perpetuate racism (Ridley, 1989). By pinpointing these defenses, counselors can take a better look at themselves and determine if they are unintentional racists.

Eight Racially Related Defenses

Color Blindness

Color blindness is an illusion that the minority client is no different from nonminority clients. Several writers have called attention to the erroneous assumption that the minority client is simply another client (Bernard, 1953; Block, 1981; Griffith, 1977; Thomas & Sillen, 1972). The ensign of color-blind counselors is a collection of phrases: "We're all the same," "I don't see you as being a minority, just another human," and "It is as though you are White."

Several factors cause color blindness. Counselors may have a strong need to appear impartial, fearing that deep down inside they are unconscious bigots. Counselors may feel uncomfortable in discussing race because it is a sensitive topic, or they may have insecurities or unresolved personal issues about race. Some counselors may be overly protective of their minority clients. In an effort to not hurt the feelings of these clients, they avoid discussing race. Other counselors may simply misunderstand minority clients. To appear competent and not expose their ignorance, they again avoid any discussions of race.

Color-blind counselors relate to minority clients as though race is unimportant. Their denial disregards the central importance of color in the psychological experience of the client. These counselors tend to overlook the influence of racism and discrimination upon the attitudes, feelings, behaviors, and personality development of minority clients. Color-blind White counselors also disregard the undeniable influence of their Whiteness upon the client (Sager, Brayboy, & Waxenburg, 1972).

The adverse consequence of color blindness is misdiagnosis. The counselor automatically labels deviations from White middle-class values as psychopathology. Counselors who do not understand the culture of their minority clients tend to look upon the clients' values and cultural idioms as inherently inferior to their own. For example, some minority clients come from cultures that value group affiliation and collectivism. Counselors stuck on rugged individualism may misinterpret the behavior of these clients as codependency. Color blindness is a major contributor to the disproportionate number of minorities assigned a pathological diagnosis.

Over the years, many professionals have consulted me about their work with minority clients. I have found that color blindness is pervasive. Usually, I try to get these professionals to consider the implications of their so-called impartiality. I often use word pictures or analogies to illustrate the consequences of looking at people apart from their social reality. I might ask, "Would your interpretation of an acting-out client change if you knew she was a victim of brutal sexual assault?" As I work my comments into a discussion of minority clients and give examples, most professionals are startled to learn that their color blindness leads to unintentional racism.

Color Consciousness

Color consciousness, the opposite of color blindness, is another illusion. It is based on the premise that the client's problems stem essentially from being a minority (Adams, 1950; Bernard, 1953; Block, 1981; Griffith, 1977; Thomas & Sillen, 1972). The color-conscious counselor places too much weight on the color of the client, while overlooking the client's contribution to the presenting problem. A counselor who surmises, "The reason you have an alcohol addiction is because you are Native American" may be color conscious.

The illusion rests on a kernel of truth, although it is still a distortion of reality. Many minorities have been subjected to oppression and discrimination. However, to conclude that they have developed an "irreversible mark of oppression" or permanently crippled personality (Kardiner & Ovesey, 1951) is erroneous. Many minorities do successfully resolve their experience with racism.

A major cause of color consciousness is White guilt. White counselors often harbor strong and painful feelings about the mistreatment of minorities in society. In some respects, they bear the burden of guilt for all White people, whether or not as individuals they are overtly racist. They use therapy to atone for their feelings of guilt about racism, even though they may not be directly responsible for any injustice.

The primary adverse consequence of color consciousness is misdiagnosis, but of the opposite nature of color blindness. Color-conscious counselors fail to identify the severity of psychopathology. They place too much emphasis on racism and the client's color. A 13-year-old Black boy was referred to me by the Department of Children's Protective Service. He came from a low-income family and had been in the system a long time. I diagnosed him as a conduct disorder adolescent. He was rebellious, antisocial, and unresponsive to adult authority. After several sessions with him, I recommended his placement in a residential treatment facility. Prior to my evaluation, color-conscious therapists probably minimized the boy's condition, enabling him to float around in the system without getting appropriate treatment.

This case teaches us that color consciousness leads to the underestimation of psychopathology. My client's conduct disorder had been overlooked by other professionals. The misdiagnosis, in turn, led to a second adverse consequence: an inappropriate intervention. The professionals should have placed the boy in a highly controlled therapeutic environment in which prosocial behaviors are consistently reinforced. This is the treatment of choice for conduct disorder adolescents.

Cultural Transference

Freud (1949) provided some original insights into the nature of the counselor-client relationship. He speculated how the dynamics of the relationship affected treatment. One of his insights was transference. He noticed that clients transfer to the therapist either positive or negative feelings and attitudes. These reactions are based upon the real feelings clients have about their parents or other significant people in their lives.

Furthermore, Freud observed that these reactions to the therapists are reminiscent of clients' earlier reactions to these important people.

As a psychology intern at a Veterans Administration Hospital, I had a firsthand opportunity to observe the effects of transference. One afternoon, a fellow intern was conducting therapy with a young woman in an office across the hall. I suddenly heard a loud commotion. The patient yelled, "You remind me of my father." Then she jumped out of her chair and began to physically assault my colleague. The psychoanalytic perspective would describe this patient's anger and hostility toward her father as being transferred to the therapist. Obviously, this case illustration is dramatic. Every counselor, though, should anticipate more subtle forms of transference.

Despite the inherent distortions in transference, Freud felt that this dynamic could be beneficial. As clients reenact their emotions and experiences, counselors have a unique chance to facilitate therapy. They can clarify and interpret psychological material that otherwise would be inaccessible to therapy. Clients can benefit by gaining new insight into their unconscious conflicts and by understanding the effects of these conflicts on their behavior and attitudes.

Cultural transference is a special category of transference. This dynamic involves the emotional reactions of a client transferred to the therapist of another race. Before entering therapy, the minority client may have had significant interactions with other members of the therapist's race. Some of these experiences may have left the client with deep feelings of resentment and hostility. At times, client reactions in counseling have nothing to do with the disposition of the therapist. Many therapists are not bigots. Nevertheless negative feelings may surface in the client because the therapist represents the majority group. The therapist shouldn't take this personally but use it as a therapeutic opportunity.

Unintentional racism may be reflected in a counselor's incompetence. Although counselors may not be the original source of a client's frustration, they may mishandle the transference. Unskilled or uninsightful counselors fail to recognize the transference. Even if they recognize the transference, some incompetent counselors minimize its psychological significance. Other counselors feel intimidated by a client's reactions and attempt to avoid dealing with it altogether. In whichever situation, the client's problems are compounded by the counselor's failure to employ constructive interventions aimed at resolving the conflicts underlying the transference. A White female doctoral student in counseling psychology became overly nondirective when a Black male client erupted into anger.

I encouraged her to take advantage of the cultural transference instead of being scared off by the client.

Cultural Countertransference

Freud (1949) also conceptualized countertransference. Like transference, he believed that this dynamic could have tremendous impact on the quality of therapy and its outcome. Countertransference refers to the emotional reactions of therapists which are projected onto clients. These reactions are similar to previous reactions to someone other than the client—a person outside of therapy with whom the counselor has had an intense emotional experience. The reactions are caused by the therapist's anxiety. The failure of these counselors to resolve their feelings results in a misperception of the client.

Cultural countertransference involves the emotional reactions of the therapist of one race projected onto the client of another race. The mere presence of the client may spark intense emotions in the therapist. These feelings are reminiscent of feelings experienced in past interactions with members of the client's race. The mannerisms, idioms, expressions, and values of the client, which seem peculiar to the therapist, may also provoke cultural countertransference.

Jones (1985) comments specifically on how therapists countertransfer onto African American clients:

> Any client can invoke in a therapist an unhelpful emotional response; what is noteworthy for this discussion is that it appears that black patients may evoke more complicated countertransference reactions and more frequently. The reason for this seems to be that social images of blacks still make them easier targets for therapists' projections and that the culturally different client provides more opportunities for empathic failures. (p. 178)

Like others who are defensive, therapists are not conscious of these feelings. Although their projections are irrational, they are reinforced by members of the therapist's race who share similar feelings and attitudes. In this state of collusion, therapists do not effectively test reality. They believe their responses are rational rather than what they really are— distortions of reality.

Cultural countertransference causes counselors to make inappropriate attributions of psychological deficiencies to minority clients. Distrust, sexual promiscuity, hostility, and Machiavellianism are prominent examples of culturally countertransferred characteristics. Sabshin, Diesenhaus, and Wilkerson (1970) observe that Black patients tend to be regarded as "hostile and not motivated for treatment, having primitive character structure, not psychologically minded and impulse-ridden" (p. 788). Once clinicians develop these false perceptions, therapy begins to lose its appropriate focus. The emphasis switches to treating an unreal person.

Some minority clients accept this invalid assessment without question. Other clients accept it reluctantly. They feel vulnerable due to the power differential in relationship to the counselor. This feeling of vulnerability almost guarantees that these clients will not challenge the counselor's assessment. Some minority clients, however, are both insightful and courageous. They protest the invalid assessment. Protesting, however, puts minority clients in a position to be further labeled as uncooperative, indifferent, or resistant.

Cultural countertransference places minority clients in a double bind. If they accept the counselor's projections, they get stuck with an inaccurate assessment. If they reject the counselor's projections, they risk having other negative labels hurled at them. The net effect of cultural countertransference is that the client's real presenting problems remain untreated.

Cultural Ambivalence

White counselors often have ambivalent motives in treating minority clients. On the one hand, they may have high power and dominance needs (Jones & Seagull, 1977). These counselors attempt to hold tight reins over the course and direction of therapy. Their need for power is motivated by insecurity, intimidation, and perhaps the perception that the client may seek reprisal for injustice. On this topic, Pinderhughes (1973) states:

> One problem area for many patients lies in the unconscious needs of many psychotherapists to be in helping, knowledgeable, or controlling roles. Unwittingly they wish to be initiators and have patients accommodate to them or to their style or approach. More Black patients than White perceive in this kind of relationship the basic ingredients of a master-slave pattern. (p. 104)

Vontress (1981) fittingly describes the high power need of White counselors as the "Great White Father Syndrome." Power-oriented counselors are condescending, paternalistic, and enraging. They tend to reinforce learned helplessness and passivity in clients. Paradoxically, this outcome contradicts one of the primary goals of therapy: assisting clients to become more responsible and assertive. The real danger is that clients will leave therapy as inept in problem solving as when they began.

On the other hand, White counselors simultaneously may be motivated by a high dependency need. These counselors expend considerable effort trying to gain the client's acceptance or approval. Beneath the approval seeking lies the desire of counselors to be absolved of guilt, whether real or imagined, for being racist. Here again counselors are working on their own issues. Jones and Seagull (1977) argue that some White professionals are motivated to counsel minorities almost completely out of their guilt about racism, probably with little help to the client.

In an earlier work, I placed counselor cultural ambivalence within the historical context of racism in America:

> This dynamic is traceable to the plantation during the antebellum period. The white master, otherwise addressed as "massa" or "massr," had a peculiar type of psychological involvement with the slave community. This involvement was characterized by both high power and dependency needs. The massa sought emotional comfort from the blacks, though relegating them to the lowest form of involuntary servitude. The blacks, in turn, catered to the massa, though bemoaning their depravity and despair in their private thoughts and gatherings. Alex Haley (1976) makes the point in *Roots* that white masters were happiest when they were around their slaves, even when they were beating them. (Ridley, 1984, p. 1239)

Cultural ambivalence has profound implications for therapy. In attempting to gain the client's approval, counselors resort to subtle manipulation of the client. Their goal is to appear nonracist and "OK" as a White person. Using subtle manipulation, these counselors attempt to prove they are different from White bigots. Without knowing it, these counselors set themselves up for the countermanipulation of the minority client, who may be keenly perceptive of the emotional dependency of the counselor (Ridley, 1984).

The consequences of the counselor's ambivalence for the client are harmful. Culturally ambivalent counselors are preoccupied with their own issues about race. As a result, they are less attuned to the psychological conflicts and unresolved issues of the client. Although the client may remain in counseling, much of the time is wasted on nontherapeutic conversation designed to alleviate the counselor's anxiety. In that sense, therapy is actually counselor-centered rather than client-centered.

Pseudotransference

Sometimes the minority client responds in a manner that appears to the therapist as defensiveness. However, these pseudotransference reactions are realistic. The client reacts strongly to the racist attitudes and behavior of the counselor. The counselor misinterprets the client's behavior and subsequently labels the client as pathological (Thomas, 1962; Thomas & Sillen, 1972). What the therapist usually ignores is the possibility that the client's critical reactions are grounded in reality. Thomas (1962) put it this way:

> Disturbed, unhealthy responses of the patient in the therapeutic situation cannot, however, be assumed to be necessarily transference phenomena. They may be "pseudo-transference" responses to unhealthy attitudes or behavior of the therapist, and therefore not an accurate reflection of the patient's neurosis. The well-known counter-transference phenomena caused by an unhealthy pattern of individual origin in the therapist can produce such pseudo-transference reactions. (p. 899)

Thomas (1962) also suggests that the client is especially sensitive to stereotyping. This experience is a repetition of everyday life. Ridley (1985b) adds that the client feels even greater vunerability because the therapist is in a powerful one-up position.

Behaviorally, pseudotransference may be depicted by a simple operant paradigm. Here antecedent (controlling) events act as discriminative stimuli (S^D) for consequent events (R), and (S^R) are reinforcing stimuli that upon presentation increase the probability of R. In the interchange sequence shown below, the S^D represents the counselor's racist behaviors; the R represents the reaction of the client; and the S^R represents the counselor's negative evaluation of the client's behavior:

A hypothetical example illustrates the paradigm. During therapy, the counselor remarks, "Why, we have a very fine Black psychologist from Harvard on our staff." This behavior is the $S^{D.}$ The remark is racist. It implies White superiority, even though the counselor has "good" intentions. The client has another interpretation. Minorities have to be superhuman to achieve parity in the White world. In reaction to the counselor's comment, the client becomes visibly annoyed but does not self-disclose his or her intimate thoughts and feelings. This behavior is the R. The client probably perceives the counselor as patronizing. Stimulus generalization may also occur, because the client has heard similar comments from Whites outside of therapy. The counselor takes careful note of the client's behavior, concluding erroneously that the client has a psychological disorder. The labeling of the client's behavior is the S^R.

The interaction between the counselor and client is actually much more complex. The S^R can acquire the S^D function. What results from this is an ongoing interaction in which the behavior of each participant is both a stimulus and a response:

White Counselor: $\quad R \cdot S^D \qquad S^R \cdot R \cdot S^D \qquad S^R \cdot R \cdot S^D$

Minority Client: $\quad S^D \cdot R \cdot S^D \qquad R^D \cdot R \cdot S^D$

Within the "interlocking paradigm" (Skinner, 1957; Strong, 1964), each response of the counselor and client is both a reinforcing (or punishing) stimulus for the immediately preceding response and a discriminative stimulus occasioning the next response. The interchange sequences involve a "chain" in terms of its sequential properties as well as its stimulus properties (Reynolds, 1968). The response of either participant increases (when the response serves as a reinforcing or discriminative stimulus) or decreases (when the response serves as a punishment or S) the frequency or probability of occurrence of certain responses by the other participant. Equally important, both participants may not be consciously aware of their response. The outcome of this interaction is that the counselor mistakenly assigns a pathological diagnosis (e.g., anxiety disorder, adjustment disorder, schizoid disorder) to the client, although in a scientific "behavioral" sense the responses of the client are justifiable.

Cultural stereotyping by White counselors has been reported in the literature. Bloombaum, Yamamoto, and James (1968) found that Mexican Americans, Blacks, Jews, Chinese Americans, and Japanese Americans, in that order, were the most frequent objects of stereotyping of practicing psychotherapists. Of the therapists' responses, 79.2% indicated subtle, stereotypical attitudes. The investigators concluded that the therapists' attitudes reflect those of the culture in general. Therefore, psychotherapists should not consider themselves immune to cultural stereotyping just because they are trained as helping professionals.

Word, Zanna, and Cooper (1974) demonstrated the power of self-fulfilling stereotypes in interracial interviews. In one study, White interviewers displayed more grammatical and pronunciation errors, spent less time, and showed less immediacy with Blacks than with Whites. Essentially, they were less friendly, less outgoing, and more reserved with Blacks. In another study, White confederates behaved in either the immediate or nonimmediate interview styles observed in the first study. White interviewees subjected to the nonimmediate styles were more nervous and performed less adequately than those exposed to the immediate style.

Snyder (1982) interprets these findings:

> Apparently, then, the blacks in the first study did not have a chance to display their qualifications to the best advantage. Considered together, the two investigations suggest that in interracial encounters, racial stereotypes may constrain behavior in ways that cause both blacks and whites to behave in accordance with those stereotypes. (p. 67)

Overidentification

Defensiveness and mishandling of minority clients are not limited to White counselors. Minority counselors also act defensively and hurt minority clients. Overidentification is one of their key defenses. To understand this mechanism, it is necessary to examine how it builds on to another defense.

Identification is a frequently cited defense mechanism (Clark, 1991). People who identify with others express admiration for and exhibit some degree of behavioral similarity to the idealized person or group (Bieri, Lobeck, & Galinsky, 1959; Lazowick, 1955). Through this association, the person gains a sense of prestige, recognition, and acceptance.

Minority counselors naturally may have much in common with minority clients. They may come from similar backgrounds. They may share similar interests and cultural values. They face some of the same challenges, such as racism, discrimination, and prejudice. Because of these shared experiences, minority counselors are in a beneficial position to identify and empathize with minority clients. When a minority student expresses frustration about being the only minority student in a physics class, the counselor may easily relate to the client. Perhaps, the counselor knows what it is like to be the only minority professional in the counseling center.

Despite this advantage, minority counselors sometimes overidentify with minority clients. They get caught up in the client's negative experiences with racism and fail to conceptualize the client's presenting problem in its total context. In much the same way that color-conscious White counselors attribute a client's problem to his or her minority status, overidentifying minority counselors develop a narrow problem definition.

Counselors who overidentify may encourage excessive discussion of race issues. These counselors provide a safe haven for minority clients to "unload" rage about White people and the racist system. Although this is appropriate to a certain extent, counselors may take it too far. They may get personal gratification out of allowing the client to unload. Counselors also may use counseling sessions as opportunities to unload their own anger and rage. They may self-disclose too much or inappropriately.

The cause of overidentification is the minority counselor's unresolved racial issues. For example, the counselor may resent being more qualified than White peers who have the same professional status. The counselor may resent having to deal with a supervisor who has limited knowledge about how to counsel minority clients. Perhaps the counselor is frustrated about getting assigned all of the difficult minority cases.

The consequence of overidentification is misdiagnosis. The counselor colludes with the client, attributing problems of the client primarily to racism. In so doing, the counselor denies the client's intrapsychic conflicts, which may be only remotely related to the client's race. As an example, a client may be the identified patient in a family seeking therapy. The deep feelings of inadequacy lead to self-defeating behaviors and prevent the client from making full use of his or her potential. Yet the client blames personal difficulties on racism, which is an easy scapegoat. A more accurate interpretation might see the client's symptomology as an expression of a dysfunctional family system. In the meantime, the underlying pathology remains unrecognized and untreated.

I once counseled a young African American man who was a Vietnam veteran. From the outset of counseling, we hit it off—partly because I am African American and partly because a special chemistry existed between us. We talked extensively about racism, both in civilian life and the military. In retrospect, I realize that I was not very helpful. Our sessions could be best described as "White establishment bashing." Months later, I ran into my former client. He appeared to be as confused as when I first began to counsel him. It then occurred to me what had really happened in counseling. Although he had been a victim of racism, he had other deep-seated issues that were never resolved. He used racism as a smoke screen. As a counselor, I colluded in his denial and hindered his progress in therapy.

Identification With the Oppressor

Some minority counselors who have difficulty in dealing with their pain associated with racism adopt another defense. They compensate by denying their minority status and identifying themselves with White people. Some writers liken this to the psychoanalytic view of the Oedipus complex, whereby a boy attempts to resolve his feelings of powerlessness by becoming like his father. This is the psychology of "if you can't beat them, join them."

Minority counselors who identify with the oppressor harbor an underlying hostility. They have self-hatred and hatred toward other members of their race. The pain of being a minority is so intense that they avoid identification with their race. Atkinson, Morten, and Sue (1993) would say that these counselors are in the Conformist Stage of their Minority Identity Development Model.

The consequence is that counselors place unrealistic expectations on minority clients. Although high expectations are important, they take it too far. These counselors judge minority clients harshly for not measuring up to White standards. They expect minority clients to make rapid therapeutic gains and penalize them for holding onto ethnic values. Their racism can be more harmful than the racism of White counselors. They counsel by the axiom, "If I can be successful in the White world, so can you." The only problem is that they define success in overly narrow terms, disregarding the fact that all minorities are not created with equal ability or potential.

I once worked with a Black psychiatrist who acted as if he hated to treat minority patients. The few Black patients that he treated seemed to hate the experience of having him as a therapist. In one case conference, the psychiatrist grilled an older Black man. I do not remember the psychiatrist ever being as harsh with a White patient. Incidentally, none of the other Black professionals had rapport with this psychiatrist.

Chapter Summary

The importance of a good relationship between counselors and minority clients was highlighted in this chapter. The relationship provides the context for helping clients achieve positive therapeutic outcomes. Numerous race-related defenses can prevent the development of a working therapeutic alliance. Eight of these defense mechanisms were discussed. Counselors who are defensive about race or fail to handle the defensiveness of minority clients were found to perpetuate racism.

Chapter 6 concludes Part I of this book. The reader should now have a solid conceptual grasp of the nature, dynamics, and complexity of unintentional racism in counseling and therapy. Part II builds on this background. Each of the following five chapters presents strategies for overcoming the counselor's unintentional racism. The emphasis is on translating theory into practice. With that objective in mind, a variety of practical interventions are described in each chapter.

Overcoming the
Counselor's Unintentional Racism

7

Counsel Idiographically

Every client is unique—each one a mixture of characteristics and qualities unlike everyone else. Clients of similar backgrounds are even different from each other. Although they have much in common, their differences outweigh their similarities. When clients arrive for counseling, they bring their personal stories, and each has a different story to tell. Because everyone is unique, counselors should not attempt to counsel every client in exactly the same way.

Counselors should realize that their effectiveness depends first and foremost on their understanding of the individual. To be really helpful, counselors must tune into their clients' personal experiences. This is the idiographic perspective.[1] It should guide the entire process of counseling. Jones (1985) underscores the importance of this perspective: "The point is that the concept of race is far too general and is not tailor-made for what is idiographically more significant to the development of a particular person" (p. 175).

This chapter describes the idiographic orientation—both what it is and how to use it in counseling. It could be argued that this is the most advantageous approach to counseling minority clients. The chapter begins with five underlying principles, followed by a case example, and then presents 12 action steps for counselors.

Five Principles

Counselors need a set of principles that serves as a general guide for counseling while respecting the individuality of each client. Five guiding principles underlie the idiographic perspective in multicultural counseling. These principles should help counselors acquire a therapeutic mindset that enables them to counsel minority clients more effectively.

1. *Every Client Should Be Understood From His or Her Unique Frame of Reference.* Carl Rogers (1961), founder of person-centered therapy, was a leading proponent of this principle. In describing the helping relationship, he characterizes the effective counselor as one who becomes acquainted with the private world of the client

> by an acceptance of this other person as a separate person with value in his own right; and by a deep empathic understanding which enables me to see his private world through his eyes. When these conditions are achieved, I become a companion to my client, accompanying him in the frightening search for himself, which he now feels free to undertake. (Rogers, 1961, p. 34)

Sometimes counselors are premature in thinking they understand their clients when they really do not. To avoid misunderstanding a client, counselors need to be empathic; they need to see the inner world of the client from the client's point of view. In applying the idiographic perspective to multicultural counseling, Ridley, Mendoza, and Kanitz (1994) state:

> The major assumption underlying the idiographic approach is that all hunches about a client that are based on prior knowledge must be considered tentative until the counselor obtains information directly from the client that either confirms or disconfirms the hunch. (p. 243)

2. *Nomothetic, Normative Information Does Not Always Fit a Particular Client.* The nomothetic perspective, in contrast to the idiographic perspective, focuses on the prominent characteristics of the group to which the individual belongs. Although the nomothetic view yields descriptions about the typical or average member of a group, any individual may deviate from the norms of the group. A strictly nomothetic approach regards the deviant person as abnormal. The idiographic perspective, however, recognizes that deviation from the norm neither implies a person is abnormal or exceptionally healthy. The person simply may be different from other

members of the group. Thus normative data may be useful but not sufficient for understanding the particular client. Counselors should look at group norms, but they should not expect to understand any client fully without exploring the individual frame of reference.

The idiographic approach underscores the need to understand the personal meaning held by the client as a *particular person,* not simply as a representative of certain groups.[2] Ibrahim (1991) argues that the application of normative information to "idiosyncratic individuals" violates their right to individuality and can be considered a form of "cultural oppression" (p. 582). Several minority professionals shed light on the importance of valuing the individuality of minority clients. Their comments, representative of descriptions of clients of other races, are found in Table 7.1.

3. *People Are a Dynamic Blend of Multiple Roles and Identities.* The notion that people have only one racial or cultural identity overlooks the uniqueness of persons. Clients are not merely representatives of a single group. They are members of a variety of groups, each overlapping in a blend that is unique and special to the individual. Pedersen (1990) states that people could have over 1,000 roles or cultures to which they belong at any given time. To better understand the individual, counselors must explore how the client's multiple roles and identities intersect to give the client unique meaning.

4. *The Idiographic Perspective Is Compatible With the Biopsychosocial Model of Mental Health.* The most comprehensive understanding of the individual is achieved through examination of the person's integrated biological, psychological, and sociological experiences. Each context contributes to an understanding of the individual, but no singular context provides conclusive understanding. The more counselors know about clients, the better they are able to help. Unlike the medical model, which primarily explores internal psychological dynamics, the idiographic perspective is concerned with a holistic view of persons. The biopsychosocial model is well-suited for this purpose.

5. *The Idiographic Perspective Is Transtheoretical.* Focusing on the individual is not constrained by a single therapeutic orientation. Instead counselors are free to adopt any therapeutic orientation and use a wide range of specific interventions. The most important rule in selecting an intervention is that client problem areas, based upon an idiographic appraisal, are specifically addressed. In this sense, individualized treatment

Table 7.1   Comments on the Individuality of Minority Clients

---

African Americans

The question "How to treat the black client?" is naively and simplistically phrased. It is as if one were asking how do we treat the narcissistic character disorder or the depressed patient. But black clients do not constitute a particular clinical or diagnostic type. Knowing that a patient is black fails to inform adequately about his views of psychotherapy, about his personality and psychological conflict, and about his aspirations and goals in therapy, let alone about educational level, social background, or environmental context. There is enormous within-group variability. The question is not how to treat *the* black client, but how to treat *this* black client. (Jones, 1985, pp. 174-175)

Asian Americans

It is essential to acknowledge that Asian Americans represent a diverse group of people with considerable between-group differences. There are over 29 distinct subgroups represented among Asian Americans. Each of these subgroups has distinct traditions, customs, and languages. Included in this population are recent immigrants and refugees from various Asian countries (e.g., China, Korea, Vietnam) as well as individuals who have been born and socialized in the United States (e.g., American-born Chinese). In addition, there are considerable within-group variations in each of the subgroups. For example, an American-born Chinese who is raised in one of the many Chinatown communities tends to be less acculturated to Western culture and values than an American-born Chinese who is raised in a rural, Midwestern town. Such differences can have significant implications for treatment. (Moy, 1992, p. 359)

Hispanic Americans

Each woman's choice expresses something about who she is as an individual as well as what her cultural values are. Superficial knowledge of Hispanic culture may lead the therapist to accept as a cultural norm what might only be the client's expression of her individuality. Conversely, a behavior that conforms to strict cultural norms or violates them at a high personal cost can be interpreted by an unknowing therapist as strictly an individual choice with no cultural implications. Cultural norms may be used inaccurately by either client or therapist to explain or excuse a woman's restricted behavior and thus prevent the exploration of other factors in the individual's life history. (Espin, 1985, p. 169)

Native Americans

The Native American population is extremely varied, and it is impossible to make general recommendations regarding counseling that apply to all Native Americans. Not only do various tribes differ from each other, but any one individual may differ greatly from other members of the same tribe. . . . A major variable is the degree of traditionalism of an individual versus the degree of acculturation to mainstram U.S. society. The continuum stretches from the very traditional individual born and reared on a reservation, who speaks the tribal language, to the Native American reared in a city who speaks only English and may feel little identification with a tribe. (Thomason, 1991, p. 321)

---

planning is the hallmark of the idiographic perspective in multicultural counseling.

The Case of Ricardo Garcia

Ricardo Garcia is a fictitious 32-year-old Mexican American male who lives in East Los Angeles. He immigrated to the United States 3 years ago in hopes of finding work and creating a better life for his family. His wife, Teresa, is 31 years old and stays at home. She spends most of her free time watching Hispanic television programs and socializing with other Hispanic women in the neighborhood. The couple has two children. Their son, Manuel, is 13 and attends junior high school. Their daughter, Selma, is 10. She is in the fourth grade. Both kids have been in bilingual classes since they arrived in Los Angeles.

Two months after Ricardo's arrival, he found a job as an apprentice to an automobile mechanic. The mechanic liked Ricardo because of his dedication and hard work. He taught Ricardo the trade, and within one year Ricardo became an expert mechanic himself, "soaking up" everything he could learn. During Ricardo's second year in the United States, he began to formally learn English as a second language. He enrolled in an evening course and showed the same intensity as he did in learning to become a mechanic. As he became more proficient in English, he developed more interest in "the way Americans do things."

Gradually, Ricardo and Teresa began to have serious problems at home. Teresa has shown little interest in branching out of the Hispanic community. The couple gets into heated conflicts, mostly over his long hours away from home and their different degree of interest in American traditions. In addition, their sex life has become dissatisfying.

To make matters worst, their children are having difficulties. Manuel is gaining acceptance by members of a Hispanic gang. A teacher at school recently called home to say she noticed a change in Manuel's attitude. Selma, who used to be outgoing, has become quiet and reserved. Now nobody really knows what she is thinking.

As Ricardo's problems escalate, he spends even more time away from home. After his evening class, he talks to Alba. She is a young Hispanic woman also learning to speak English. He knows there is an attraction between them, but his strong Catholic beliefs tell him not to get involved.

An Idiographic Conceptualization of Ricardo

After an intake interview, counselors may find themselves overwhelmed by the complexity of Richardo's story. They may ask a number of questions about the case such as the following.

- How typical are Richardo's problems among Hispanic males?
- To what extent are Ricardo's problems attributable to his cultural adjustment, racism, or his own psychological issues?
- Do counselors need specialized training to counsel this type of client?
- Are there particular interventions that are suited for this type of client?
- How does one effectively assess Ricardo?

To begin to answer these questions, counselors should look at Ricardo idiographically. The case material suggests eight cultural roles that can aid counselors in taking their idiographic look. Ricardo is a Mexican American, a man, father, husband, Catholic, mechanic, student, and resident of East Los Angeles. See Figure 7.1 for an idiographic conceptualization of Ricardo.

Although Richardo has many roles, there is more than one way to attempt to understand him. Counselors can look at Ricardo as though he has a predominant role such as a Mexican American or resident of East Los Angeles. But each role examined separately offers a limited view of what it means to be Ricardo as a unique person. Counselors can also attempt to understand Ricardo as he appears in his various roles. If they want to see the total picture, they should explore Ricardo's unique frame of reference based upon conjoint membership in eight roles.

To get an insightful look at Ricardo, counselors should focus their attention on the center of the diagram. This center section represents Ricardo's idiographic experience or, as Robinson (1993) suggests, the "indivisible intersection." It is his uniqueness as a person having eight cultural roles. Viewed from this perspective, Ricardo's idiographic experience sets him apart from every other Mexican American, man, father, husband, Catholic, mechanic, student, and resident of East Los Angeles. None of these roles should be overlooked, however, for each contributes in some way to an understanding of him.

Possible Interpretations of Ricardo

Here are three possible idiographic interpretations of Ricardo. Any one of these interpretations may be true of him, or each may be a misinterpretation. These descriptions illustrate how counselors can look at the same

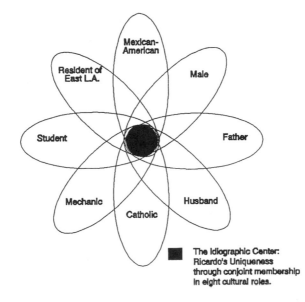

Mexican-
American

Resident of
East L.A.

Male

Student

Father

Mechanic

Husband

Catholic

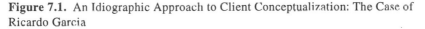

The Idiographic Center:
Ricardo's Uniqueness
through conjoint membership
in eight cultural roles.

Figure 7.1. An Idiographic Approach to Client Conceptualization: The Case of Ricardo Garcia

client and case material and yet arrive at different interpretations. This also demonstrates why counselors must learn how to counsel idiographically. It helps them become more proficient in understanding their clients.

Interpretation 1

Ricardo is fed up with his marriage and family responsibilities. He feels that he has worked hard to improve his life, and his reward for all the hard work is nothing but trouble. He resents Teresa because she is lazy and not motivated to help them get ahead. He blames her for the children's problems. He believes she wastes too much time on TV and friends when she could be helping their kids. He likes talking to Alba because, unlike Teresa, she also wants a better life. He also thinks that if Teresa put her religion into practice, she would be more motivated.

Interpretation 2

Ricardo is scared and feels guilty. His mother always wanted him to be a priest. In his poor Mexican village, the priest was looked upon as the person to turn to for help. Although being a mechanic is a good way to earn a living, this job is not as important as being a spiritual guide and helping people. Ricardo now wonders if his problems are punishment for not following the call into priesthood. He feels he has let down a lot of people— first his mother and God and now his wife and children. He also feels guilty talking to Alba about his problems because he should be able to talk to Teresa about them.

Interpretation 3

Ricardo is confused and ambivalent. On the one hand, he has always been a devout Catholic. Because of his strong Catholic faith, he tried to take care of his family, attend Mass regularly, and be faithful to his wife. He even detested the macho stereotype of Hispanic males. On the other hand, Ricardo is struggling with some new attitudes. He doesn't like to feel "trapped at home." He questions the value of religion because it "doesn't work anymore," and now he is sexually attracted to Alba. And although he likes life in this country, he wonders whether he is "selling out." Ricardo feels pulled in opposite directions. The only thing that doesn't bother him is his job as a mechanic.

Therapeutic Actions

To counsel minority clients idiographically, counselors can initiate the following 12 actions. Each action is described.

1. Develop Cultural Self-Awareness

Most people have strong cultural biases, values, and expectations, and counselors are no exception. Yet most counselors do not realize how their feelings and attitudes affect counseling, especially as they attempt to understand clients of different races or cultures. Therefore, they should become self-aware. Unless counselors take a good hard look at themselves and examine their personal agendas, they are likely to ignore, distort, or underemphasize a client's idiographic experience.

Race is a sensitive topic, arousing strong feelings in people. Counselors should try to find out if they have hidden attitudes or biases that limit their objectivity. Rosen and Frank (1962), two White psychiatrists, claim that few people are free of racial prejudice. Wintrob and Harvey (1981) argue that counselor self-awareness is important for effective cross-cultural psychotherapy. Jones (1985) goes a step further, suggesting that self-awareness is the only way to prevent counselors' personal reactions from intruding in unhealthful ways.

One way for counselors to develop cultural self-awareness is to get personal counseling. Rogers (1961) asserts that counselors must be congruent if they are to be helpful. Congruent counselors are aware of their feelings, attitudes, and perceptions at a conscious level. Because of their self-awareness, congruent counselors can deal with their issues without projecting them on to their clients.

Ridley (1989) suggests that counselors should get counseling from a therapist of another race—especially one who is skilled in multicultural counseling. Ideally, the therapist of choice should be of the same race as the major client population served by the counselor. This is the racial group most vulnerable to the counselor's countertransference. The purpose of counseling is to help counselors identify and work through their biases and prejudices, again alleviating themselves of the need to countertransfer. On this subject, Axelson (1993) states that becoming aware of hidden prejudices is the first step in promoting an open-minded counseling relationship.

2. Avoid Value Imposition

Not only should counselors identify their biases, they must be careful not to impose their cultural values on their clients. To put this recommendation into perspective, therapist neutrality is widely held up as a therapeutic ideal. According to Freud (1912/1963) and many practicing analysts who continue to hold his views, the "neutral" analyst serves as a blank screen on which patients can transfer intense emotions and reactions. Coonerty (1991) states that psychoanalysts believe that the real person of the therapist is of negligible influence.

Therapist neutrality is seriously questioned. Katz (1985) states that therapy, instead of being value free, is connected to the social, political, and historical realities of the counselor's culture. Along similar lines, Draguns (1989) argues that culture is an invisible and silent participant in counseling. But counselors may not recognize the inevitable presence of culture. Wrenn (1962, 1985) coined the popular phrase "cultural encapsulation" to depict the disposition of counseling students and faculty who are unaware of their cultural biases.

So what role do counselors' values play in counseling? According to Kelly (1990), who reviewed the literature on values in counseling, counselors tend to impose their values on clients even when they do not intend to do so. He adds that counselors judge progress in counseling by the degree to which clients adopt their values. The implication for multicultural counseling is serious. Counselors unknowingly expect minority clients to become like them.

Counselors should make a conscientious effort to avoid value imposition. To accomplish this task, they need to identify their values. Edward Hall (1973) describes 10 basic categories of values in every culture. Every counselor should become familiar with this list.

- Language—verbal message systems and communications
- Temporality—attitudes toward time, routine, and schedule
- Territoriality—space, property
- Exploitation—methods of control, use, and sharing of resources
- Association—family, kin, community
- Subsistence—work, division of labor
- Bisexuality—differing modes of speech, dress, conduct
- Learning—observation, modeling, instruction
- Play—humor, games
- Defense—health procedures, social conflicts, beliefs

In each category, counselors should isolate their personal values and the values of their clients. If their values are similar to the client, the chances of value imposition are slim. If their values are different from the client, counselors should determine how important it is for the client to change values.

3. Accept Your Naiveté as a Multicultural Counselor

Counselors are highly trained professionals who are regarded as psychological experts. They are trained in assessment and intervention planning. A few are multicultural experts, skillful in counseling clients from other races and cultures. No counselor, however, is initially an expert on the individual.

Counselors need to get to know their clients before they can be helpful. During the early phases of treatment, counselors may get hunches or formulate hypotheses about their clients. But counselors are often wrong. Because their hunches and hypotheses may not hold true, counselors should be tentative and proceed with caution. They should replace the automatic information processing style often employed with members of their own race with a more cautious information processing style. This style enables counselors to consider the unique cultural makeup of the client. It also gives counselors the opportunity to check out the goodness of fit of their hypotheses with each client. Even experienced counselors should take this posture.

Maintaining a naive posture is not easy, especially because counselors are socialized to play the role of expert. Yet they really do not have a choice. They should commit themselves to this posture and work at proceeding cautiously with each client. Only when counselors accept the limits of their expertise are they likely to make more realistic interpretations of their clients.

4. Show Cultural Empathy

Cultural empathy is the ability of counselors to understand and communicate the concerns of clients from their cultural perspective (Ridley, Mendoza, & Kanitz, 1994). Cultural empathy has two dimensions: understanding and communication. Understanding involves getting at the heart of the client's idiographic meaning. Culturally empathic counselors unclog their perceptual filters of cultural bias. Communication involves conveying to the client the counselor's understanding of the client's idiographic experience. This means that counselors use language that is meaningful to the client. Here are some ways to become more culturally empathic.

First, do not fake your understanding of the client. If you are unsure of what the client is trying to say, ask for clarification. There are numerous cultural expressions and idioms that may be unfamiliar to counselors. Counselors are not expected to know every word or phrase used by clients of different races or cultures. However, they should not hesitate to seek clarification when they do not understand a client. Here is an example of a cultural clarification.

> **Counselor:** You have used the phrase "deuce and a quarter" several times. Could you please give me an example of what you mean by this?

Second, invite the client to ask for clarification of what you say. Sometimes counselors use professional language that is unfamiliar to minority clients. Many clients are embarrassed to admit they do not know what the counselor means. Set the stage early in counseling for clients to freely ask for clarification. Here are two invitations for clarification.

> **Counselor:**   We counselors sometimes use professional language that our clients don't understand. Because counseling is a new experience for you, feel free to ask for clarification if I use a word that is unfamiliar to you. This should help us both to better understand each other.

> **Counselor:**   You seem puzzled by something I've said. Tell me what I said that was puzzling, and I'll try to be more clear.

Third, ask for illustrations from the clients' cultural experience. Sometimes clients have difficulty expressing themselves. They might find it easier to communicate their idiographic experience by giving real life examples or illustrations. Here are two ways counselors can facilitate communication.

> **Counselor:**   Describe the most vivid situation you remember when you felt like you were out of place with both Whites and other Blacks.

> **Counselor:**   Tell me about a time when you were trying to figure out if Whites really accepted you or just needed you around as the token minority.

5. Incorporate Cultural Considerations Into Counseling

Many counselors behave as though the cultural background and experiences of minority clients are irrelevant to understanding them as unique persons. However, the failure to include culture in the therapeutic formula adversely affects many aspects of counseling. Several authors assert the value of exploring cultural issues in treatment, especially when the concerns of the client relate to racism and discrimination (Atkinson, Thompson, & Grant, 1993; Casas, 1984; Thompson et al., 1994; Vargas & Koss-Chioino, 1992).

Ridley, Mendoza, Kanitz, Angermeier, and Zenk (1994) clarify the value of using culture in counseling:

> All therapy is culturally contextualized, and positive therapeutic outcomes depend on the skillful incorporation of cultural considerations into the basic design of counseling intervention. Conversely, behaving as if culture is irrelevant is countertherapeutic. Such behavior results in an inadequate understanding of individuals and an inability to maximally assist them in achieving therapeutic goals. (p. 128)

These authors continue by arguing that attunement to cultural variables promotes an increase in therapeutic leverage, opening up greater opportunities to understand the needs, concerns, personal goals, and adjustment of clients.

A case from my training experience illustrates the importance of accommodating counseling interventions to the cultural experience of minority clients. A counselor on campus asked a young Japanese woman many questions concerning dating patterns and male-female relationships in Japan. The questioning was extensive and time-consuming. After the counselor finished this line of inquiry, he continued to counsel the student as though he never collected this information.

The counselor made two mistakes. First, he did not personalize the cultural information to the client. He sought to find out about Japanese women in general but not this client in particular. It should have been of interest to the counselor to discover how dating patterns and male-female relationships in Japan impacted the client's life as a student at an American university. Second, the counselor did not translate his quest for information into therapeutic goals or interventions. The counselor simply wasted time because the information was not used to help the client.

Counselors must be purposeful in gathering and incorporating culturally relevant information. They must be alert to cultural data during all phases of counseling. They must also incorporate cultural considerations into every therapeutic activity, whether it is problem identification, diagnosis, goal setting, treatment planning, termination, or referrals. Otherwise, they may end up with clients who are puzzled and disappointed, who drop out of counseling early as did this Japanese student.

6. Do Not Stereotype

Stereotyping is a simplified, generalized labeling of a group of people. Snyder (1982) points out several popular stereotypes: Italians are passionate, Blacks are lazy, Jews are materialistic, and lesbians are mannish in demeanor. Stereotypes in general can be distinguished from racial preju dice, which is a special category of stereotyping. Unlike a stereotype, racial prejudice implies bigotry. Prejudiced people always stereotype, but people who stereotype are not necessarily prejudiced. Brown (1965) argues that stereotypes are inevitable and necessary coping mechanisms that allow people to avoid cognitive overload. Stereotyping or (overgeneralizing) helps people to package a variety of stimuli impinging upon them into a manageable number of categories. Although many stereotypes are inaccurate, others contain a "kernel of truth."

McCauley, Stitt, and Segal (1980) point out that stereotypes have negative repercussions when people use them to make predictions about others but do not attempt to gain more information before making the prediction. Stereotyping is particularly spurious when (a) characteristics are assigned to people because they are assumed to be inferior, (b) stereotypes lead to a "self-fulfilling prophecy," or (c) people who stereotype are dogmatic and unwilling to open themselves up to new information that might contradict their beliefs. Once rigidly formed, stereotypes are highly resistant to change (Axelson, 1993).

Counselors should attempt to identify their stereotypes. Atkinson, Morten, and Sue (1993) describe the stereotype of Asian Americans as high achievers who experience few emotional and social problems. These authors point out how school counselors holding this positive stereotype might discriminate against a student. Counselors might assume that the Asian student needs academic and career counseling but not personal counseling. Without exploring other dimensions of the student's experience, counselors may allow their preconceived mental picture to dictate what is important for the student. What the student may need the most, such as working through some emotional issues unrelated to career and academic concerns, may not fit a counselor's stereotype.

Gerrard (1991) provides a graphic case of a Black student who was stereotyped by her high school guidance counselor. She put her experience this way:

> He just took one look at me and it's just like, "Great, not only is she a girl but she's Black. Everyone knows like it's hard enough to find smart Black people, let alone smart Black girls." Basically, that was the assumption he was working under. (p. 562)

The student's impression of the counselor was based on several factors: his attitude toward her, his tone of voice, and his comment that she could not go into medicine or get a scholarship. He offered no reason for his conclusion. His body language also communicated lack of interest. "He was just sort of sitting there as if bored out of his skull, waiting for me to say something" (p. 562).

Gerrard (1991) suggests that this is not simply the case of a pragmatic counselor attempting to be realistic with the client. At least, the counselor could have said something like "Here are the barriers. Are you prepared to overcome them to get what you want" (Gerrard, 1991, p. 562). Instead, he stereotyped her based upon her sex and race.

7. Weigh and Determine the Relative Importance of the Client's Primary Cultural Roles

It is essential for counselors to gain an understanding of a client's idiographic center or personal frame of reference. Failure to truly understand clients as unique persons precludes the possibility of counselors taking the most appropriate course of action. More than likely, these counselors will select inappropriate interventions.

Counselors must remain open. They must examine the major cultural roles of a client and how these roles contribute to the client's idiographic experience. In some cases, they will find that a few roles are heavily influential in understanding a particular client. In other cases, counselors will find that many roles are of more equal influence. The point is that it is practically impossible to know beforehand how a client's multiple roles uniquely contribute to his or her idiographic experience.

Counselors are reminded that effective counseling involves intense therapeutic work. Understanding a client seldom occurs with one easy cut, and it is almost impossible to completely understand someone else. Nevertheless, counselors must examine and reexamine the client's cultural roles without overemphasizing or underemphasizing the contribution of any one role. In the case of Ricardo Garcia, it would be premature to assume that his Mexican Americanness is any more or less important to his idiographic experience than being a Catholic or a mechanic. His Mexican Americanness is one of many dimensions of his experience, although it may be very important for understanding him. With this in mind, counselors should actively check out the relative importance of each of his roles.

8. Do Not Blame the Victim

Being a victim in a racist society is tragic. Being a victim of racism twice—first in society and again in counseling—is more of a tragedy. Counselors who strictly hold to the medical model and disregard the biopsychosocial model are almost certain to victim-blame minority clients. Their reactions, to quote Corey et al. (1993), result from "tunnel vision."

Counselors need to continually educate themselves, no matter how long they have been in practice. To overcome the tendency to blame the victim, take these steps.

- Review your assessments of minority clients. Periodically—every quarter or half a year—reexamine the case notes of these clients. See if a pattern of psychopathology exists in your clinical judgments. Find out what factors go into your assessments. See if your decisions are based upon intrapsychic factors, environmental factors, or a combination of the two.

- Compare your assessments of minority clients with those of White clients. Determine if differences exist in the types of judgments you make about the two groups of clients. If differences exist, examine your case notes to find out what factors lead to your decisions for each group.

- Get feedback on your cases. Ask supervisors or other professionals with multicultural expertise to go over your cases with you. From time to time, present one of your minority clients in a case conference where colleagues can examine your assessment and treatment planning.

- Try to ascertain if you use cultural countertransference—that is, blame minority clients for your own unresolved racial issues. You may take this step in conjunction with getting personal counseling, as recommended earlier. Be on the alert for hostile feelings and sexual idiosyncracies, which are projections common among counselors who culturally countertransfer.

9. Remain Flexible in Your Selection of Interventions

Because every client is unique, counselors need to be flexible and use a variety of interventions. They should not use the same interventions repeatedly just because they have a favorite counseling orientation. Rather they should select interventions that are suited to the unique needs and problems of the client. If counselors put the needs of clients first, there will be times when they have to forgo using their favorite interventions.

Some counselors believe that fairness means using the same interventions with minority and nonminority clients. They wrongly assume that equal treatment means equitable treatment. Sue (1977) was probably the first professional to recognize and challenge this assumption. He argued that equal treatment in counseling might mean discriminatory treatment. On the other hand, he asserted that differential treatment does not necessarily imply discriminatory treatment. Because equal access and opportunity for all clients is the real issue, Sue favors the use of differential techniques that are nondiscriminatory. Sue's position makes a great deal of sense, if one accepts the definition of racism proposed in this book.

To achieve flexibility, Ridley (1984) and Ponterotto (1987) recommend multimodal therapy for treating minority clients. According to Lazarus (1989), multimodal therapy encompasses a variety of techniques without allying itself with a specific therapeutic orientation. Lazarus identifies six modalities which constitute human personality: behavior, affect, sensation, imagery, cognition, and interpersonal relationships. He also identifies a seventh nonpersonality modality, drugs (or medication). Lazarus coined the acronym BASIC ID, derived from the first letter of each modality.

Counselors who use multimodal therapy can systematically employ a broad repertoire of interventions. They are not confined to interventions that may be inappropriate or unhelpful. Instead, they can select interventions addressing the needs of clients in each modality.

Ponterotto (1987) provides a good hypothetical case using multimodal therapy with Francisco, a Mexican American male. Francisco presented a number of problems, each of which Ponterotto matched to one of the modalities, proposing a specific treatment. For example, Ponterotto identified the client's lack of assertion at a local city agency as a behavior problem and then proposed assertive training, role playing, and self-as-a-model treatment. Ponterotto added another problem area to the regular profile, which he called *Interaction with Oppressive Environment.* One of his proposed interventions for this problem area was the development of a plan of action to pressure the city agency to hire Spanish-speaking employees. See Table 7.2 for Francisco's Modality Profile. This case demonstrates why flexibility is one of the most important requirements for effectiveness with minority clients.

10. Examine Your Counseling Theories for Bias

Most major theories of counseling and psychotherapy originated in Eurocentric ideology. Like all theories, they are predicated on assumptions and presuppositions. The relevance of these theories to minorities and Third World people has been seriously questioned by a number of scholars. Holiman and Lauver (1987) described the counselor's theoretical orientation as one of several "filters" that distort the counselor's perception of the client.

To use traditional counseling theories beneficially with minorities, counselors need to evaluate them for cultural bias. Pedersen (1987, 1994) identifies ten assumptions, reflecting cultural bias in counseling. They are:

- a common measure of "normal behavior"
- emphasis on individualism
- fragmentation by academic disciplines
- dependence on abstract words
- overemphasis on independence
- dependence on linear thinking
- neglect of client's support system
- focus on individual versus system change
- cultural encapsulation
- neglect of history

Table 7.2   Francisco's Modality Profile

Modality	Problem	Proposed Treatment
Behavior	Lacks assertion at local city agency	Assertive training Role playing Self-as-a-model
	Behavior directed by what others (city agency) might think or say	Rational disputation Counselor modeling
Affect	Strong feelings of anger, frustration, guilt, and worry	Counselor support Anger management Rational discussion
Sensations	Tension headaches and stomach pains	Relaxation training Biofeedback Abdominal breathing exercises
Imagery	Images of uncomfortable scenes at city agency	Desensitization Positive imagery
Cognitions	Negative self-talk and self-blaming	Rational disputation and corrective self-talk Thought stopping
Interpersonal relation	Negative family interaction	Preventive rational discussion Substitute coping behavior training
Interaction with oppressive environment	Oppressive environment influences	Counselor *acknowledges* oppressive environment. Client and counselor develop an organized plan of action to pressure city agency to hire a member of the Spanish-speaking community. Counselor explores (through referral contacts) other options (e.g., Are there comparable Spanish-speaking agencies that could handle client's financial concerns?).
Drugs/Biology	Tension headaches and stomach pains	Physician consult if symptoms persist

SOURCE: Reprinted from Ponterotto, J. G. (1987). Counseling Mexican Americans: A multimodal approach. *Journal of Counseling and Development (65)*6, 308-312. Copyright © American Counseling Association. Used with permission of the publisher.

Using Pedersen's 10 assumptions, Usher (1989) evaluated client-centered theory for its cultural relevance. She found that six assumptions underlying the theory are culturally biased. The biased assumptions are an emphasis on individualism and independence, a here-and-now time orientation, minimal focus on external influences, abstract constructs that are meaningless or offensive to minority clients, and a narrow theoretical foundation. Usher's critique of Rogerian theory is an excellent model for examining cultural bias in other theories. The critique is particularly noteworthy in light of Rogers's strong idiographic stance. If cultural bias can be found in his theory, the relevance of other theories to minorities can certainly be questioned.

Ivey, Ivey, and Simek-Morgan (1993) examine the major theories of counseling and psychotherapy from the multicultural perspective. Their work is a helpful reference for counselors wanting to critique these theories. Ridley, Mendoza, and Kanitz (1994) suggest a technique for examining theories for their cultural relevance. The technique involves identifying key issues and assumptions of these theories. Counselors can use this analysis to develop their own multicultural theory of counseling.

11. Build on the Client's Strengths

A major criticism of multicultural counseling is the tendency of counselors to concentrate almost exclusively on the weaknesses of minority clients. Certainly, minority clients may have serious presenting problems. But they also have many strengths and tremendous potential. While vigorously looking for psychopathology, counselors miss many opportunities to help clients identify their assets and use these assets advantageously. All clients need to realize that they have assets.

To help clients build on their strengths, counselors have several options. First, they should look for the positive side of so-called dysfunctional behavior. As previously demonstrated, not all behavior judged as a problem is actually dysfunctional. In an early writing on race in therapy, Rosen and Frank (1962) describe how behavior can be reframed positively:

> The Negro's position as a member of a minority group subjects him to experiences which differ from those of the white of corresponding socio-economic status, and the therapist must evaluate the patient's history with this in mind. Intermittent school attendance or frequent change of job may indicate not emotional instability but the effort to survive. Nor need a jail sentence have the same implications for a Negro as for a white patient. (p. 459)

Here is an hypothetical situation—the client who has frequent job changes. The counselor should affirm the client's motivation and effort to survive instead of characterizing him or her as unstable. Perhaps, the client's best attempt to cope with racism, poverty, and inadequate education necessitates moving from one menial job to another. The fact that the client is motivated to work and persistent in seeking gainful employment should be regarded more favorably than the erratic work history. Once counselors see this as an asset, they should try to figure out how to help the client make better use of this personal resource.

Second, counselors should identify past accomplishments of the client. Some minority clients, especially those from poor backgrounds, may underestimate their potential. Sensitive counselors affirm achievements that minority clients do not see or regard as small or insignificant. I worked with an African American teenager who was a member of an inner-city gang. He was streetwise and influential among his peers, but he knew right from wrong. His dream was to become a lawyer, and I saw tremendous potential in him. I assisted him in getting into college. Although he did not complete his education, he became a police officer, working with inner-city youth. His savvy and experience, coupled with the confidence he gained by going to college, enabled him to excel at his job.

Third, counselors can teach new behaviors or encourage clients to get training in specialized areas. Vocational training, marriage enrichment, and assertiveness training are examples of areas in which clients might acquire new skills. The important point is that counselors can start by helping clients at their existing level of functioning and then cultivate other skills for personal enhancement.

12. Do Not Protect Clients From Emotional Pain

Most clients are motivated to get relief from emotional pain. This is their No. 1 priority, even at the expense of making constructive change. Minority clients are no different from other clients in this respect. Counselors can get so taken up in the client's quest for pain relief that they also make this the priority of counseling. What counselors and clients both may fail to realize is that pain associated with healing is inevitable.

Some counselors are extremely sensitive to the pain experienced by minority clients. They know that these clients face racism and discrimination, plus other social problems. They have a genuine feeling of concern, and they try to make counseling as painless as possible. Despite their good intentions, these counselors make a tactical error. They choose interventions that are painless but not helpful.

One of my clients was a very attractive African American woman. She was in her mid-30s and was a successful corporate executive. Although this client was a competent professional, she was unsuccessful in dealing with her emotional pain. Her personal life was like a horrid drama in which she moved from one abusive relationship to another. I asked her what she got out of choosing men who abuse her. At first, she denied any responsibility and shifted the blame to the men in her life. As I continued to press her, we discovered that as a child she received very little attention and approval from her father. As an adult, any attention she received, even if it was negative, became rewarding. In her eyes, it was better than no attention. She had never come to terms with the pain she felt of emotional abandonment from her father. We facetiously called her numerous forays with men the "replacement strategy." It was a reminder of her dysfunctional way of dealing with emotional pain.

Pain often accompanies healing. Melzack and Wall (1982) state that pain can be a signal to prevent serious injury, prevent further injury, or set limits on a person who has been seriously injured. Counselors do their clients a disservice when they try to protect them from therapeutic pain. They must employ interventions that work, even if this makes their clients uncomfortable. Counselors should adopt this motto: "Effective interventions first and client comfort second."

Chapter Summary

Minority clients must be treated as individuals and not simply as members of their race. While acknowledging the importance of race and culture, counselors are encouraged to develop an idiographic understanding of minority clients—their unique personal meanings as experienced through multiple cultural roles and identities. Twelve action steps were presented in hopes that counselors become more effective in treating minority clients as individuals.

Notes

1. The terms *idiographic* and *nomothetic*, first proffered by Windelband, were popularized by Gordon Allport (1946). These two approaches to the study of personality are widely used in psychology and are not limited to counseling and psychotherapy.

2. Studies in differential psychology consistently demonstrate that within-group differences are larger than between-group differences. This finding applies to a variety of behavioral, personality, and cognitive variables. For authoritative discussions on the topic, refer to Atkinson, Morten, and Sue (1993, Chap. 2), Bronstein & Quina (1988), and Zuckerman (1990).

8

Set Culturally Relevant Goals

The success of counseling ultimately depends upon setting and achieving goals that are tailored to the needs of clients. Clients benefit most from counseling when goals are realistic and attainable. The worst scenario is for no goals to be set at all. Although goal-setting does not guarantee success, it increases the chances that counseling will be successful. Goal setting also enables counselors to evaluate counseling. Evaluation, in turn, enables counselors to change their strategies when necessary—again improving the chances of successful counseling. Cormier and Hackney (1993) offer a helpful perspective on the importance of goal setting in counseling:

> Goals give direction to the therapeutic process and help both counselor and client to move in a focused direction with a specific route in mind. Without goals, it is all too easy to get sidetracked or lost. Goals help both the counselor and client to specify exactly what can and cannot be accomplished through counseling. (p. 103)

Counseling involves two types of goals: process and outcome goals. Both are critical to the success of counseling. Process goals are concerned with therapeutic movement and the conditions necessary for clients to change. Typically, they involve the interaction between counselors and clients. Outcome goals are changes expected to be made by clients as a result of counseling. These include changes in behavior, attitudes, and feelings. The idiographic perspective makes it clear that each client should have a unique set of outcome goals.

Setting culturally relevant counseling goals is the subject of this chapter. The discussion includes both process goals and outcome goals. Most of these goals are added to other goals that might be set in counseling. The process goals should be incorporated in every counseling case. The outcome goals, however, may not be equally relevant to every minority client. Counselors should check against this list to determine which ones are appropriate in particular cases.

The Need for Collaboration

Someone must take responsibility for goal setting in counseling, although opinions vary as to whom. One position holds that counselors are responsible. It could be argued that they have the psychological training and expertise to determine what goals serve the best interests of clients. Another position holds that clients are responsible. It could be argued that clients are experts on themselves and therefore capable of determining what goals serve their own best interests.

Both of these extreme positions have merit. However, there are serious drawbacks to each. Counselors may know psychological theory and how to apply clinical interventions, but they do not begin counseling as experts on individual clients. Their lack of expertise on minority clients compounds the problem. On the other hand, clients know themselves better than anyone else. But many of them are caught up in dysfunctional behavior, pain avoidance, and secondary gains. This unhealthy stance blinds them to how counseling may be most beneficial.

To maximize the assets and minimize the liabilities of the counseling participants, goal setting should involve a joint effort. In short, counselors and clients should collaborate. Collaborative goal setting has other advantages. Minority clients gain a sense of empowerment and ownership of the counseling process. This is important because minorities often feel powerless, and nothing will happen if they do not own the goals. Counselors gain early insight into minority clients, a difficult achievement for some counselors.

The best way to collaborate is for counselors to directly ask clients to participate in goal setting. Some minority clients will readily respond to this request. Others who are unfamiliar with counseling will be more reluctant. Still others will blatantly resist collaboration. Counselors should explain to minority clients how vital their input is to the success of counseling.

The Counselor's Unstated Goal

Achieving equitable outcomes with all clients should be the priority of every counselor. This should also be the most important criterion for determining success in overcoming racism. As counselors improve their service delivery, increasing parity between minority and White clients should exist in the areas of diagnosis, staff assignment, treatment modality, utilization, treatment duration, and client attitudes toward treatment. From an open systems perspective, the change from inequitable to equitable outcomes can be depicted as follows:

$$\frac{\text{Majority Group}}{\text{Minority Group}} \quad \Longrightarrow \quad \text{Majority Group} = \text{Minority Group}$$

Equal outcomes across racial groups may be difficult to achieve. It might be more realistic to think in terms of achieving approximately equal outcomes, because many complex variables are involved in multicultural counseling. Nevertheless counselors should make every effort to provide fair and equitable service delivery, to monitor their work, and to revise their interventions when this is necessary.

Process Goals

Three process goals should be of interest to counselors who counsel minority clients: establishing a working alliance, exploring the racial dynamics between the counselor and client, and obtaining a counseling agreement.

1. Establish a Working Alliance

The most important process goal is to establish a working alliance with the minority client. Every counselor, regardless of therapeutic orientation, should set this goal as a priority. Without this goal, counseling cannot move forward. Gelso and Carter (1985) define the working alliance as the alignment or joining together of the client's reasonable or observing side with the counselor's working or "therapizing" side. This definition could be reframed, suggesting that clients and counselors are process observers of counseling, as well as active participants of change. The stronger the working alliance, the more likely counseling will benefit the client.

The working alliance reflects the effort and commitment of both counseling participants. Clients must be permitted to "stand back" and reasonably observe what is happening within the counseling relationship and within themselves. They must also be able to experience their emotions, including negative feelings toward the counselor. Counselors must commit themselves to working wholeheartedly in the interest of the client. They should conduct themselves professionally, abide by ethical principles, and employ scientifically based interventions.

Gelso and Fretz (1992) state that trust is the client's most important contribution to the working alliance. But trusting a counselor is often difficult for minority clients. They may not trust White counselors or the counseling process. Sometimes they do not fully trust minority counselors, feeling that these counselors have sold out to the White establishment. A common theme of mistrust of White counselors has been reported among African Americans, Asian Americans, Hispanic Americans, and Native Americans (Everett, Proctor, & Cartmell, 1983; Gomez, Ruiz, & Laval, 1982; Sue & Sue, 1990; Vontress, 1981).

Overcoming the minority client's mistrust is the greatest contribution counselors can make to the working alliance. They must be authentic in the relationship. Counselors must be alert to themes of concealment, suspicion, and disguise. They must seize every opportunity to demonstrate that they are for the client. When a client makes a therapeutic gain, counselors can show strong affirmation. Perhaps when a client is really struggling, counselors can send a note of encouragement between sessions.

2. Explore the Racial Dynamics Between the Counselor and Client

Closely related to establishing a therapeutic alliance is the need to determine how the client's attitudes about race affect counseling. Ethnicity has been equated with sex and death as a subject arousing deep unconscious feelings in most people (McGoldrick, Pearce, & Giordano, 1982). Added to an already complicated process, racial dynamics ensure that counselors face a major challenge. But how can counselors sift through the psychological nuances to determine the racial attitudes of the client? How are counselors to distinguish distortions due to cultural transference from realistic reactions of clients?

First, counselors should realize that many minority clients enter counseling with a certain amount of fear and anxiety. To some of these clients, White counselors represent symbols of oppression. To some of these clients, minority counselors are seen as people who can no longer relate to the minority experience. Counselors should remember that deep-seated fears and hostilities underlie these attitudes.

Counselors must accept their clients' anxieties and encourage them to openly express their feelings. Counselors should not discourage or penalize their clients for disclosing threatening information. It is a contradiction to encourage clients to be open and then penalize them for doing what they were asked. Accepting a client's anxiety means that counselors first accept their own anxiety provoked by the client. Counselors must be honest with themselves about their apprehension and discomfort. While being congruent about their feelings, they should be sensitive enough to not provoke more anxiety in the client. Counselors should remember that the counseling setting is inherently threatening to many minority persons.

Second, counselors should explore their clients' racial attitudes early in treatment (Spurlock, 1985; Sykes, 1987). Some minority clients are not bothered by the race difference between themselves and the counselor. If race is not a major issue for the client, counselors should not harp on it but move on to other issues. Other minority clients are deeply troubled by the race differences. According to Jones and Seagull (1977) and Jones (1979), race differences probably have their greatest impact early in treatment, particularly during the first session. If counselors sense that racial dynamics are affecting the client, they should explore these issues in depth. The failure to explore these issues can block progress in therapy as well as minimize the possibility of the client being receptive to positive interracial experiences in the future (Ridley, 1984).

If counselors sense that racial dynamics might influence counseling, they can use interventions such as the following.

Counselor: Many clients who come to counseling for the first time do not know exactly what to expect. Some are threatened by the situation. The fact that you and I are of different races may make you even more uncomfortable or question whether I can really help you. If you have these feelings, let's try to get them out in the open. We can make better progress that way.

Counselor: You stated on your intake questionnaire that you are having conflicts in the residence hall, and you used the word *ignorant* to describe some of the students. I know that your experience growing up on the south side of Chicago is very different from many of our students who grew up in suburban and rural communities. I feel badly that not everyone is as sensitive as they should be. I think we should begin counseling by talking about your recent conflicts and what it means to you to be a Black student in a predominantly White university.

Exploring race is not easy. Jones (1979) notes that minority clients may try to test the therapist. They are wary of counselors and want assurance that they will be accepted. Once again, counselors must create a supportive environment. By giving support, counselors can demonstrate that minority clients can be vulnerable with a concerned counselor of another race. These positive experiences may also help minority clients overcome the tendency of generalizing racism to all White people (Ridley, 1984).

Third, when it seems appropriate, counselors should share some of their own feelings with the client. Egan (1994) points out several benefits of counselor self-disclosure. It may serve as a form of modeling, create intimacy between the counselor and client, and send an indirect message to the client: You too can self-disclose. Counselors should not overburden clients with their anxieties, but they can allow clients to see that they too are vulnerable. Consider the following counselor self-disclosure.

> **Counselor:** I sense that talking about this issue might be difficult for you. I want you to know it is not real comfortable for me to talk about race. This is a sensitive topic, and I don't want to be misinterpreted. It is important, though, that we get these issues out into the open. If we avoid talking about race, even though it is uncomfortable, we might not accomplish our goals.

The type of counselor self-disclosure is crucial. In discussing the clinical treatment of the nondisclosing Black client, Ridley (1984) gives an example of both insensitive and sensitive disclosures:

> When I was in elementary school, one of my best friends was a black boy named Ralph.

and

> I was unemployed for six months after I finished my Ph.D.; I just couldn't find a job. (p. 1241)

Sensitive disclosures, as in the latter example, are authentic and reflect interest in the client's concern. Unlike insensitive disclosures, they help to create a climate of trust and often encourage minority clients to share their feelings.

3. Obtain a Counseling Agreement

Cavanagh (1982) suggests four areas in which counselors and clients need to reach an agreement: the practical aspects of counseling, roles, expectations, and goals. Practical aspects include the frequency of sessions, the length of sessions, the policy regarding cancellation and missed appointments, and billing procedures. Roles include such things as whether a counselor adopts a more directive or reflective counseling style or how much the client should focus on the past versus the present. Expectations include issues such as honesty, commitment, and effort to reach counseling goals, priority placed on counseling, and doing homework assignments. Goals—as we discuss in this chapter—should be specific, measurable, realistic, attainable, and capable of being owned by the client.

The importance of obtaining an agreement becomes clear when one considers the consequences of the lack of structure in counseling. Sue and Sue (1972) point out that the counseling situation is intentionally ambiguous. The counselor listens empathically and responds only to encourage the client to talk more. Haettenschwiller (1971) indicates that racial/ethnic minority clients frequently find the lack of structure confusing, frustrating, and even threatening. Preference for a directive counseling style over a nondirective style has been found among many Asian American college students (Atkinson, Maruyama, & Matsui, 1978), Japanese American young adults (Atkinson & Matsushita, 1991), Native American high school students (Dauphinais, Dauphinais, & Rowe, 1981), Mexican American community college students (Ponce & Atkinson, 1989), and Black students (Peoples & Dell, 1975).

Gong-Guy, Cravens, and Patterson (1991) explain the importance of clarifying treatment expectations with Southeast Asian refugees. These people associate mental health treatment with severe psychopathology that requires permanent institutionalization. Thus they tend to shun treatment or use it as a last resort when family, traditional healers, and medicine prove ineffective. When refugees do show up as clients, they may expect medication on the first visit and interpret the need for repeated visits as a sign of ineffective treatment.

Clearly misunderstanding between counselors and clients on the style of counseling can hinder progress in counseling. Counselors need to be extra vigilant in clearing up differences in roles and expectations with minority clients. I have found it helpful to begin new counseling relationships with a *structuring introduction*. In many ways, this sets the tone for therapy. I introduce a number of topics, including my philosophy of healing and change, my orientation to counseling, legal and ethical considerations, and practical aspects of counseling. I invite clients to share their goals and expectations. I also invite them to ask me for clarification of my agenda. Finally, I try to find out how the cultural expectations of minority clients match up with my usual counseling procedures. Many clients appreciate my attempts to collaborate with them and take the mystery out of counseling.

The Case of Nor Shala

The following is an actual case illustration. It is presented in the words of the client. The difficulties she experienced in an intake interview illustrate why it is important for counselors to attend to the three process goals: establishing a working alliance, resolving racial dynamics, and obtaining a counseling relationship.

Somewhere in the first week of this semester, I decided to see a counselor at the health center. So, I called them and told them that I preferred a woman counselor. I was very apprehensive because I have never seen a counselor before in my whole life. Nevertheless, I gave myself a try because I was desperate to see someone who could help me with my problem.

At the counseling center, a lady counselor somewhere in her late 30s introduced herself to me and brought me to her room. Before that, I had filled in a form asking information about my general background. In the room, the lady counselor asked me to sit in a chair while she was busy reading the form that I had just filled in. Then she asked me, "What is your problem and why are you here?" The minute I opened my mouth, she quickly wrote down something with her face facing downward but not at me. I thought she was not yet ready to listen to me, so I stopped talking. But, while holding her pen and looking downward at her paper, she told me to go on. I personally feel weird talking to someone who doesn't even look at my face. I feel like I am talking to the wall.

I did not know where to start my story or what I should talk about in order for her to understand me. So, many times after talking to her for a few sentences, I stopped. The counselor did not asked for clarification of certain points or even indicate to me if she understood what I was saying. When I stopped, she asked me to go on. While writing down everything, she'd say, "Go on. I am taking down what you are saying so that I can figure out things here." I was hoping that she would stop writing and try to reword what I said and then give me her interpretations of what my problem is.

Toward the end, she said, "I understand your problem. I know it is very stressful on your part. But, I don't know much about Muslim culture. Just in the last two weeks, I read a short paragraph about Islam." At that point, I was feeling very ambiguous. She was not focusing specifically on my problem, which has nothing to do with me being a Muslim. I was telling her about the differences in the background between me and my husband. Although we are both Malaysian, I graduated from a university in the United States but my husband graduated from a Malaysian university. So we hardly communicate with each other because of the different meanings/interpretations that we have on some issues that we discussed.

She told me to come again because she needed to hear more before she could figure out what is my problem. While she was telling me that, her eyes kept looking back and forth at the clock hanging on the wall behind my back. Her behavior prompted me to ask her this question, "How long should this session take?" Then, she quickly answered me, "Oh, it's fifteen minutes." At that point, I realized that I had taken about 17 minutes. I apologized to her because I did not know. When I talked to my classmates in the cross-cultural counseling class, they told me it was only an intake session. I asked them what is an intake session. Only then did I understand why the lady did not say much to me. My suggestion would be that she should have told me from the very beginning that this is only an intake session, and that she needed to write down some of the information that I told her. In addition, she should have told me how long this session should take rather than "hinting" to me that the time was over. I felt embarrassed about the "time" incident. I feel no sense of sincerity on her part. To me, what was more important to her was time and the procedure rather than the content of the problem. I would suggest that she focus on *my* problem not myself as a Muslim woman. In addition, she did not even realize that I am Asian. I also hoped she would comfort me by telling me in her words what my problem is and by convincing me that I need to talk more in a longer session in the future so that she can help me sort out my problem. There are a lot of technical problems here.

I will never go back to the counselor again because of my feeling of distrust on the counseling process. Actually, if someone really knew how to show that she is concerned, I think Asians would appreciate that. In my culture, we really appreciate someone who is willing to listen and help us. That person will be perceived like "part of us."

Outcome Goals

Three outcome goals should be of interest to counselors who counsel minority clients: resolution of racial victimization, bicultural competence, and antiracism assertion.

1. Resolution of Racial Victimization

Racial victimization leaves minorities with an invisible wound. This wound, although invisible, is testimony of actual trauma. Steele (1990) considers memory to be the powerful wound of racial victimization:

> I think one of the heaviest weights that oppression leaves on the shoulders of its former victims is simply the memory of itself. This memory is a weight because it pulls the oppression forward, out of history and into the present, so that the former victim may see his world as much through the memory of his oppression as through his experience in the present. (p. 150)

According to Steele (1990), unresolved memory has several debilitating effects. First, it causes victims to distort reality, sometimes with gross exaggeration. There is a propensity for victims of racism to attribute the cause of any problem to racism. In this state of denial, even the remotest cue may trigger a feeling of victimization "by connecting events in the present to emotionally powerful memories of the enemy" (Steele, 1990, pp. 153-154). If a minority experiences conflict with an employer, he or she may automatically connect it to someone else who was a racist. The present conflict, however, may not have anything to do with racism.

Second, unresolved memory leads to a reenactment of the victimization role. Shackled by self-doubt, fear, and helplessness, many minorities forgo opportunities to exploit their potential and opportunities, choosing to reenact their past victimization. The secondary gains of this reenactment involve avoidance of the consequences of relinquishing the victim role. The fear of confronting racism head on, the threat of discovering one's true abilities in a free but competitive society, the scorn of other minorities who choose to forsake their freedom—these and many other avoided consequences are the real benefits of remaining in the racial victim role.

Third, unresolved victimization results in a denial of personal responsibility. Steele (1990) offers this insight:

> But most of all they reinforce the collectivism of inversion by always showing black problems as resulting from an oppression that can only be

resisted by collective action. And here is where the distinction between societal change and racial development is lost where the individual is subsumed by the collective. . . . The price blacks pay for inversion, for placing too much of the blame for our problems on society, is helplessness before those problems. (p. 163)

Resolution of racial victimization requires skillful interventions. The interventions should logically flow from the dynamics of the problem. One therapeutic strategy is to challenge the minority client's distortions of reality.

> **Counselor:**   I've noticed that every time you bring up a new problem—whether it's your academic studies, part-time job in the bookstore, or intramural basketball—you end up saying that your failures are due to the racist system. I do not want to make light of your feelings or the real injustices that exist on campus. But is it possible that your constant focus on racism actually distracts from some deep feelings you have about being an ethnic minority?

In confronting the client, the counselor tries to ascertain the extent to which the client exaggerates racism as a problem. The counselor wants to find out whether the client has a legitimate complaint or unresolved racial conflicts manifested in blaming the system. The counselor must be sensitive to the meaning and experience of racism. With some minority clients, the problem is more complex, involving a confluence of the client's reaction to real racism and unresolved racial victimization. The clinical picture is complicated by a mixture of a healthy reaction to racism and a skillful use of racism as a defense mechanism. The therapist must balance support for that portion of the client's experience that is truly the result of racial victimization and confrontation of the portion that results from unresolved memory.

Here is a counselor's attempt to sort out the nuances of racial meaning.

> **Counselor:**   As I listen to you, I'm wondering if there might be two problems. One is that there are some instances in which you really do get the brunt of other people's racial insensitivity. Some of your experiences don't seem like they would happen except for the fact that you are Black. The other problem is that you tend to see many of your difficulties through the eyes of memory. What I mean is that because you really have been hurt, you may think racism is always the source of your problems. Is it possible that both of these are true?

Another therapeutic strategy is to directly challenge the racial victim role. Counselors must show minority clients that the victim role is self-fulfilling. As long as minorities cling to secondary gains, they do nothing to step outside of their racial victim role. They may inadvertently provoke defensive responses from people they fear as being racist. To initiate a challenge, a counselor might say this.

> **Counselor:**   There is a certain amount of comfort in being a victim. It connects you to all other members of your race who are victims. And I know that is important. But what are the risks for you choosing not to be a victim anymore? It might test your real ability to succeed in college without blaming every problem on racism.

One other strategy is to encourage individual responsibility. Once disarmed of defensiveness and the racial victim role, minority clients are free to exploit their opportunities and move beyond helplessness. Counselors should do everything possible to equip these clients with problem-solving skills. Here is a counselor challenge.

> **Counselor:**   No one said it is going to be easy. Of course, you may encounter some racism on campus, and of course, you are going to have to work hard. But let's try to examine your strengths and weaknesses, and let's see how you can make the best use of the resources on campus. You are the only one who can pursue your own goals.

2. Bicultural Competence

Most minorities continually face the conflicting values and demands of two worlds: their own communities and the dominant White society. Their interactions are not limited to people of their race. Many of their activities such as work, schooling, recreation, and personal business take them outside of minority communities. Their involvements necessitate numerous transactions across cultures. Therefore, an important goal for minority clients is to learn to function effectively both in the majority society and in the minority community. Phinney, Lochner, and Murphy (1990) argue that minorities must assert their own ethnic values and traditions without rejecting those of the majority. They must revitalize and strengthen aspects of their culture that have been devalued by the majority. The figure depicts the ongoing challenge minorities face in negotiating two worlds:

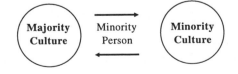

To successfully negotiate two worlds, minorities pay some handsome psychological dues. The experience can lead to considerable stress, tension, and frustration. This stress is especially severe among minority students attending predominantly White schools (Mabry, 1988; Rousseve, 1987) and immigrant families, where traditional parents clash with acculturating adolescents (Arax, 1987; Szapocznik & Kurtines, 1980). Phinney et al. (1990) describe several coping strategies of minorities:

- Alienation/marginalization: "Individuals accept the negative self-image presented by society, become alienated from their own culture, and do not adapt to the majority culture" (p. 57).
- Assimilation: "Individuals attempt to become part of the dominant culture and do not maintain their ties with their ethnic culture" (p. 59).
- Withdrawal or separation: "Individuals emphasize their ethnic culture and withdraw from contact with the dominant group" (p. 60).

Each of these responses has negative mental health implications.

Phinney et al. (1990) describe a more healthy response, biculturalism. "Individuals retain their ethnic culture and adapt to the dominant culture by learning the necessary skills" (p. 61). De Anda (1984) defines bicultural competence as the ability to understand and step in and out of two cultural environments. This is achieved by adjusting to the norms of each culture as a means of attaining one's objectives. W. E. B. DuBois (1969) explains this manner of adjustment among African Americans:

It is a peculiar sensation, this double consciousness, this sense of always looking at one's self through the eyes of others, of measuring one's soul by the tape of a world that looks on with amused contempt and pity. One ever feels two-ness—an American, a Negro; two souls, two thoughts, two unreconciled strivings; two warring ideals in one dark body, whose dogged strength alone keeps it from being torn asunder. (p. 45)

Beverly (1989) discusses the relevance of dual consciousness to clinical treatment:

One such technique is the use of dual consciousness, a concept that suggests that black clients must be able to navigate, orchestrate, and negotiate life in two worlds—one black and one white—and that success depends upon one's ability to function effectively in both. Black Americans have been forced to assess their social reality according to their primary point of reference—the black community and a broader reference—European-American culture. The two cultures rarely, if ever, merge; thus the competing and often contradic-

Table 8.1   Traditional Afrocentric and Eurocentric Values

Basic Values	Afrocentric	Eurocentric
Time	Present/here and now	Future
World views	Systemic, holistic	Linear
	Spiritual	Materialistic
	Group/community	Individualistic
	Harmony	Mastery
Identity	Self and community	Self
Acquisition of knowledge	Gained through introspection and faith	Known by measuring
Transmission of knowledge	Oral expression	Ichnographic

SOURCE: Anderson, L. P. (1991). Acculturative stress: A theory of relevance to Black Americans. *Clinical Psychology Review, 11*(6), 685-702. Copyright © 1991. Reprinted with kind permission from Elsevier Science Ltd., The Boulevard, Langford Lane, Kidlington OX5 1GB, UK.

tory imperatives of the two cultures create the need for dual consciousness. For the practitioner, dual consciousness means that all communications must be delivered and received at two levels—the inner reality of being black and the outer reality of living in a society in which being black interferes with opportunities for creative development, transcendence, and redemption. (p. 374)

To further understand the challenge of bicultural competence, consider the inherent conflict between traditional Afrocentric and Eurocentric values. See Table 8.1, which is representative of the differing value orientations of minorities and Whites. Of course, not every African American is deeply Afrocentric, and not every White American is deeply Eurocentric. Nevertheless, most African Americans and other minorities regularly confront Eurocentric values. There is not a similar press for most Whites to negotiate minority cultures in order to survive.

Bicultural competence is necessary for the adjustment and survival of most minorities. Although it is often stressful to negotiate life in two worlds, the benefits of bicultural competence outweigh the liabilities of incompetence. Szapocznik, Scopetta, Arnalde, and Kurtines (1978) found that Cuban immigrants who could negotiate both worlds have the best psychological adjustment. Biculturally competent children demonstrate greater role flexibility and creativity, have higher self-esteem, show greater understanding, and have higher achievement levels than others (Ho, 1992; Ramirez, 1983).

To focus a discussion on bicultural competence, counselors could intervene in this way.

> **Counselor:** Your life takes on many dimensions, some of which are quite different from each other. You relate to your Latino family and friends in your community. You also work in a predominantly White office downtown. We need to explore how you can be successful in both places without sacrificing one for the other.

Obviously, minority clients vary considerably in their biculturality. Counselors should help each client to determine in what ways and how much change is needed. Once clients realize the benefits of improved bicultural competence, they should make it a part of their lives. LaFramboise, Coleman, and Gerton (1993) describe six skills of the biculturally competent person. These skills are (a) knowledge of cultural beliefs and values, (b) positive attitudes toward both majority and minority groups, (c) bicultural efficacy, (d) communication ability, (e) role repertoire, and (f) a sense of being grounded. The authors' discussion of these skills should be of invaluable assistance to counselors who are attempting to facilitate bicultural competence among minoritgy clients.

3. Antiracism Assertion

Most minorities encounter racism in one form or another. Some deal with it assertively. Others do not. Still others react with aggression. An important goal in counseling is to train minority clients in antiracism assertion. Assertion refers to using behaviors that protect one's own rights without interfering with the rights of others. Three general classes of behavior fall under the rubric of assertiveness: (a) refusals to acquiesce to the request of others, (b) expressions of opinions and feelings, and (c) expressions of one's own requests (Christoff & Kelly, 1985).

Assertiveness reduces one's anxiety. Assertive people express their feelings and thoughts honestly, make socially appropriate responses, yet consider the feelings of others (Masters & Burish, 1987). Assertion is distinguished from aggression, which is hostile and coercive and disregards the needs of others.

There are many situations in which minorities can assert themselves against racism. Here are a few.

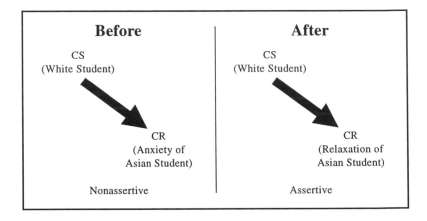

Figure 8.1. Assertiveness Training of an Asian Student

- when they are expected to play the role of the "model minority"
- when they have to perform better than Whites to get equal recognition and rewards
- when they hear racial slurs or derogatory comments
- when someone implies that a minority's accomplishment is due to his or her minority status but not competence
- when they are excluded from equal access and opportunity

The basic mechanism of change in assertion is direct exposure to the threatening stimulus. But it is common for people to avoid threatening situations, precluding the possibility of change. Like other classical change procedures, assertion rests on the premise that two incompatible responses cannot coexist simultaneously. A person cannot be both anxious and not anxious. To overcome their anxiety in a racist situation, minority clients must assert themselves by facing racism, standing up for their rights, and refusing to be mistreated.

Consider an Asian student in high school who is teased about her slanted eyes by a White student. A nonassertive response is to say nothing and avoid the White student as much as possible. The Asian student's anxiety is a conditioned response (CR) to the White student, who acts as a conditioned stimulus (CS). Because the White student is a previously neutral stimulus—one that does not naturally invoke anxiety—the Asian student can learn to overcome her anxiety about the White student. This is achieved by asserting herself. She might say something like this: "Your comments are unkind and insensitive. I don't have to accept your ignorance. If this continues, I will report you to the principal." Behaving assertively tends to reduce the student's anxiety because assertion and nonassertion are incompatible responses. See Figure 8.1.

Counselors can facilitate assertiveness using a variety of techniques. They might begin by encouraging minority clients to talk about the types of situations where they experience racism. Then counselors could model assertive responses. Next counselors can employ behavioral rehearsal where the client has opportunity to practice assertion in the safe context of the office. This also allows the client opportunity to receive feedback from the counselor. The ultimate goal is to transfer the client's assertive behavior learned in counseling to actual situations where racism is experienced.

In the following example, the counselor models assertive behavior.

Counselor: Let me model for you what to say and then you can practice it on me. "I refuse to accept your disrespectful comments anymore. If you cannot appreciate differences in people, then you have a problem. If you don't stop it, I'll report you to the administration."

Chapter Summary

Counselors improve their chances for success by setting realistic and attainable goals and collaborating with clients to achieve these goals. In this chapter, culturally relevant process and outcome goals were examined. These goals are important to both the adjustment of minority clients and success of therapy. They are added to other goals usually set in counseling. Counselors, in collaboration with minority clients, should determine which goals are most appropriate in particular cases. Consistent with the idiographic perspective, the goodness of fit of each outcome goal for individual clients is paramount.

9

Make Better Clinical Decisions

To improve the overall quality of their service delivery, counselors must improve their clinical decision making. Sound clinical judgment and case conceptualization are the hallmark of effective interventions. The prevalence of racism in the mental health field makes the need for sound clinical judgment all the more pronounced.

Improving the quality of clinical decision making does not occur automatically. Counselors should be aided by well-founded guidelines. Otherwise, they will more than likely continue to make numerous judgmental and inferential errors.

The focus of this chapter is on improving the counselor's decision making. The discussion is divided into two major sections: general strategies and personal debiasing strategies. In reading this chapter, counselors should discover the need to be more deliberate and expand their range of considerations when making clinical decisions.

General Decision-Making Strategies

Four general strategies can help clinicians improve the quality of their decisions: broadening their view of assessment, particularizing their assessments, using multiple methods of data collection, and interpreting test scores cautiously.

1. Broaden Your View of Assessment

Many counselors have a narrow view of assessment. Their view is typically limited to psychological testing or diagnosis. Spengler (1992) departs from the narrow view. He defines assessment as "all activities engaged in by the counselor in which the counselor forms an impression, or a hypothesis about the client" (p. 4). Assessment is more than hanging a label on a client. It involves developing a comprehensive picture of the client as a unique person.

This broader view of assessment is consistent with the biopsychosocial model of mental health. As counselors begin to redefine their perspective of assessment, they will include a broader range of counselor decision-making activities and methods for gathering data about clients. Therefore, the traditional image of counselors administering a test or battery of tests or painstakingly trying to find the most suitable diagnosis falls short of this assessment perspective. Counselors should be open to exploring any information that helps them to better understand their clients and select treatment strategies.

2. Particularize Your Assessments

When it comes to assessing a client, there is a tendency among clinicians to make sweeping generalizations. Kadushin (1963) found that intake workers are prone to write general diagnostic reports. These descriptions often fail to differentiate one patient from another. Along similar lines, Jones and Thorne (1987) note that subjective experience is often deemphasized in multicultural assessment. Malgady, Rogler, and Costantino (1987) comment on this problem in the mental health evaluation of Hispanics: "Without an individualized approach to culturally sensitive assessment and diagnosis, the unsuspecting clinician can easily be led down the proverbial well-intentioned pavement of the path to hell—cultural sensitivity is not stereotypy" (p. 233).

Thoughtful and accurate assessment of the particular client is essential. Competent clinicians are not simply concerned about normative data or well-worn clinical clichés. It is too easy to describe an Asian client as "restrained" or a Hispanic male as "macho." It is also easy to say that a minority client "has blunted affect," "is disoriented to time, person and place," "shows inappropriate behavior," or that the "data contraindicates severe psychopathology." Although these statements may be true in some cases, they are too nondescript for meaningful treatment planning with most clients. Clinicians should be interested in the "rediscovery of the subject" in intercultural assessment (Jones & Thorne, 1987).

3. Contextualize Your Assessments

Although the focus of assessment is directed toward gaining an idiographic understanding of the client, clinicians must remember that behavior always exists in some context. The contextual view purports that behavior can only be understood within the context in which it occurs. Szapocznik and Kurtines (1993) extend the concept of contextualism based upon their work with Hispanic youth and families. Their model embraces the notion of embeddedness. The individual is seen as embedded within the context of family within the context of culture. Moreover, cultural contexts are seen as diverse and complex, requiring individuals to develop bicultural competence. Szapocznik and Kurtines's (1993) model is an excellent reference for understanding the complexity of cultural demands placed upon minority clients.

4. Use Multiple Methods of Data Collection

Because clinical assessment is wrought with pitfalls, clinicians should use a variety of assessment methods. The advantage of one method can compensate for the disadvantage of another. Of course, there are numerous assessment procedures available, and some discretion is needed in the selection of these procedures.

Dana (1993) provides an extensive discussion of multicultural assessment. He divides assessment methods into two categories. Methods that study the individual intensively include (a) behavior observations; (b) life histories, case studies, interviews; (c) accounts; (d) life events; (e) picture-story techniques and tests; (f) inkblot techniques and tests; and (g) miscellaneous methods such as word associations, sentence completions, and drawings. Methods that compare examinees to others include (a) broadspectrum and single-construct psychopathology measures, (b) personality measures, and (c) major tests of intelligencies and cognitive functions. Dana gives examples of the various methods with specific application to minority populations.

A detailed discussion of assessment procedures is beyond the scope of this book. Interested readers are referred to Dana (1993), Jones and Thorne (1987), and Westermeyer (1987). Several suggestions, however, could guide multicultural assessment. First, clinicians should become familiar with the strengths and weaknesses of the various methods. This will be helpful in deciding which methods to use. Second, clinicians should be committed to an integration of data. A carefully constructed picture of the client should be drawn from the various sources of information. Third, clinicians should remember that each assessment method provides a limited amount of information. No single procedure is adequate for obtaining a comprehensive idiographic perspective of a client.

5. Interpret Test Scores Cautiously

Test scores indicate *how well* individuals perform at the time of testing, but they do not indicate *why* they perform as they do (Anastasi, 1992). Consequently, test scores yield imprecise information about examinees. Imperfection in testing increases when ethnic and racial minorities are tested. For example, the average performance of minorities on intellectual abilities tests can differ as much as a standard deviation below Whites (Helms, 1992).

There is always an imminent danger that counselors will misinterpret test scores. Counselors must recognize the inherent bias against minorities in much of testing. The question then is: How should counselors interpret test data without biasing their interpretations against minorities?

Here are several concepts from test and measurement to help counselors. Every test consists of a relationship among three elements:

X = the score obtained by an examinee who takes a test

T = the "true" or actual amount of the attribute or trait possessed by the examinee

E = the amount of random error involved in the testing.

Kaplan and Saccuzzo (1993) state that classical test theory assumes that every examinee has a true score that would be obtained if errors were not present in measurement. Because tests are imperfect, however, the examinee's observed score may differ from his or her true ability or characteristic. This difference between the true score and obtained score results from measurement error. Therefore, an examinee's obtained score (X) can be considered a combination of "truth" (T) and error (E). The more reliable a test, the more the obtained score reflects truth. The less reliable a test, the more the obtained score reflects error. The following symbolic representation depicts the relationship among the three elements:

$$X = T + E$$

Many counselors mistakenly use tests as though they are free of error. This leads to misinterpretation. Counselors often interpret test scores as though they perfectly represent the actual amount of the attribute possessed by the examinee. They mistakenly operate off of the following implicit formula:

$$X = T$$

To better understand why X does not equal T, consider this illustration. Suppose a young man weighs himself on a scale. He is completely disrobed except for a pair of cowboy boots and shorts. He forgot his contact lenses, so his visual acuity is off. In addition, a spring in the scale is worn, causing it to lose some of its tension. The young man reads his weight as 173 pounds. However, this is a misinterpretation. His real weight is 165 pounds. The young man does not realize several sources of error leading to his misinterpretation: the extra weight of his cowboy boots, his visual deficiency, and the reduced tension in the spring.

Paper and pencil tests are subject to more sources of error than a mechanical scale. By definition, an error is any trait or condition that is irrelevant to the purpose of testing and produces inconsistencies in measurement. A number of writers have addressed the special sources of error in the testing of ethnic minority examinees (Dana, 1993; Helms, 1992; Reynolds & Brown, 1984; Samuda, 1975). After accepting the imprecision of test scores, counselors are ready to make more cautious interpretations. They should apply all of the other general decision-making strategies in conjunction with this method.

Case Example. Jon Hawkeye is a 13-year-old Navajo Indian. He travels to and from school 45 minutes each day because he lives on a remote part of the reservation. He has been learning to speak English for the past 5 years in school, but he speaks his tribal language when he returns home.

The school district administers a testing program to place students in "appropriate" learning environments. Jon arrived at school and took the WISC first thing in the morning. Jon was sleepy because he woke up at 6 a.m. to walk a half mile to catch the school bus. He was unfamiliar with some of the words on the test because they are never spoken in his area of the reservation. Also, he was frustrated by the objective approach to testing. He is used to story telling and the oral tradition as a way of conveying information.

Jon scored 88 on the test. Average is considered to fall between 90 and 109. School counselors who only look at the test score might conclude that Jon is low average or borderline. But examiners who consider the potential sources of error in testing might arrive at a more cautious interpretation. It is possible that Jon is average or above average. Counselors should familiarize themselves with testing concepts such as standard error of measurement and standard error of estimate. This will help them make more careful interpretations of test scores.

Personal Debiasing Strategies

Debiasing strategies help counselors reduce the chances of making judgmental and inferential errors. Here are four such strategies.

1. Investigate Alternative Explanations of Client Behavior

It is easy to get stuck on one explanation of behavior. Counselors should avoid getting stuck, because they are often wrong. A better strategy is to consider alternative explanations. This should help counselors to arrive at correct explanations of behavior more often.

Gold and Pearsall (1983) showed the importance of ruling out hypothyroidism as a factor in depression. Research has found hypothyroidism to be etiologically significant in approximately 15% of the cases of major depression. The *Diagnostic and Statistical Manual of Mental Disorders,* Third Edition Revised (*DSM-III-R*), requires clinicians to rule out organic factors before making a diagnosis of major depression.

Counselors who do not rule out an organic hypothesis run the risk of making a misdiagnosis. Spengler, Strohmer, Dorau, and Jard (1994) speculated that counseling and clinical psychologists rarely test a thyroid hypothesis. They tend to overlook the condition even when there are clear symptoms suggesting hypothyroidism.

As victims of racism, alternative explanations for the behavior of minority consumers are often overlooked. Counselors routinely should investigate a host of possible etiological factors. Racism, dietary deficiency, socioeconomic conditions, health care, educational conditions, vocational and career opportunities, and social support are some of the areas counselors can investigate.

Black students, more than any other group, are likely to be mislabeled as learning disabled or emotionally handicapped (Committee for Economic Development, 1987; Reed, 1988; Rivers, Henderson, Jones, Ladner, &

Williams, 1975). With these labels, they are more likely to be placed in special education or nonacademic tracks. Professionals should know, however, that the majority of cases of mental retardation fall within the mild range and can be attributable to environmental factors. Goldstein, Baker, and Jamison (1986) report impoverished living conditions, poor health care, and lack of cognitive stimulation as such factors. Professionals who rely primarily on a hereditary explanation of intellectual development not only overlook important etiological factors but fail to provide the most appropriate educational and psychological interventions.

2. Consider Probability and Base Rate Data

A base rate represents the proportion of individuals from an identified population who share certain characteristics or features. Unless counselors are aware of these features, they may confound their decisions. If counselors know base rate data before hand, they can integrate this information into their decision making. Consider these base rates derived from epidemiological research: 1 out of 4 women and 1 out of 8 to 10 men are sexually abused as children (Finkelhor, 1984).

Base rates increase in certain diagnostic disorders. Bemporad, Smith, Hanson, and Cicchetti (1982) reported that the rate of childhood trauma may rise as high as 85% in individuals diagnosed with a Borderline Personality Disorder. Schonbachler and Spengler (1992) found that clinicians are either unaware of these higher base rates of childhood trauma, or they overshadow the presence of sexual trauma secondary to the more salient borderline profile.

To avoid misdiagnosis, counselors must consider base rate data. This consideration should be prominent in the diagnoses of minority clients. For example, stress is considered a causal factor in the declining health and emotional well-being of many African Americans. Kessler (1979) and Mueller, Edwards, and Yarvis (1977) found that Blacks experience undesirable events more often than Whites. Blacks have also been found to require more adjustment than Whites to life-changing events such as employment, family and economic problems, and death of a friend (Komoroff, Masuda, & Holmes, 1968; Wyatt, 1977).

The reported incidence of severe forms of psychopathology and personality disorders is highest among Black Americans, especially Black males (U.S. Department of Health and Human Services [USDHHS], 1986). Professionals who diagnose psychopathology among Blacks, no doubt, fail to factor in the comparatively higher stress in this population. Furthermore, they are unfamiliar with the added burden of acculturative stress brought about by the confrontation of Afrocentric values with Eurocentric values (Anderson, 1991). This analysis is not to suggest that psychopathology does not exist among Blacks. Of course, it does. These findings suggest, however, that responses to stress among Blacks have a higher probability of being misdiagnosed as psychopathology. Counselors must familiarize themselves with base rates of specific disorders to reduce the chances of misdiagnosis.

3. Use Both Confirmatory and Disconfirmatory Hypothesis Testing Strategies

Counselors want to maximize making true positive and true negative decisions. At the same time, they want to minimize making false positive and false negative decisions. It is important to avoid making a diagnosis and sticking with it regardless of the fact that more information disproves it. To help make this possible, counselors should employ confirmatory and disconfirmatory strategies.

Confirmatory strategies are attempts to confirm or validate the clinician's initial hypothesis. If an adolescent is believed to have a conduct disorder, a counselor might place the adolescent in a situation with social rules to test the hypothesis. For example, the counselor could give the client assignments between counseling sessions, help the family structure rules at home, and consult with teachers on their expectations. If the adolescent is noncompliant and rebellious, this may confirm the hypothesis.

Disconfirmatory strategies are attempts to disconfirm or invalidate the clinician's initial hypothesis. Faust (1986) states:

> Clinicians would often do much better if they tried actively to disconfirm hypotheses rather than to support them. If one can find strong evidence that one's hypothesis is wrong, which may not be found unless one looks for it, one has a better chance of uncovering the right conclusion. (p. 427)

Consider the same adolescent hypothesized to have a conduct disorder. A counselor could apply the diagnostic criteria in the *DSM-IV* to rule out the diagnoses. The counselor could look for a repetitive and persistent pattern of aggressive conduct, violating the rights of others, or a major violation of age-appropriate societal norms or rules (American Psychological Association, 1994). Specific criteria include at least three of the following: aggression to people and animals, destruction of property, deceitfulness or theft, and serious violations of rules. If clients fail to meet one or more of these exclusionary criteria, the counselor has a stronger basis for disconfirming the conduct disorder hypothesis.

Morrow and Deidan (1992) offers several other precautions gleaned from the literature. Counselors should:

- ask both confirming and disconfirming questions of the hypotheses and diagnosis
- remain open to information that seems to contradict their initial impressions
- generate reasons why their hypotheses may be wrong
- make their impressions explicit by writing them down

This may help counselors clarify their assumptions and biases.

Competent counselors try to confirm and disconfirm their hypotheses. They recognize the complex nature of clinical decisions. They also recognize that a balanced approach to decision making minimizes the chances of making false positive and false negative decisions.

4. Delay Decision Making

Before counselors can be certain about many of their decisions, they must engage in complex decision-making processes, like those we have mentioned. They need to allow a period of time to be uncertain before they can become certain about their decisions. Thus, they need to maintain decision uncertainty.

First, they should form tentative hypotheses. It is natural to form initial hypotheses and get first impressions. Everyone does. Counselors should be encouraged to begin to formulate hypotheses early in counseling. But they should recognize that hypotheses are just that—perceptions and preliminary statements of truth, not facts. The problem lies in counselors treating clients as though their hypotheses are true. Sometimes the counselor's hypotheses are true. Often the counselor's hypotheses are wrong. It is in the best interest of the client for counselors to formulate tentative hypotheses until they gather more information to test them out.

Second, counselors should delay decisions and making final judgments about clients. Although decision making in counseling is unavoidable, premature decision making should be minimized. Counselors are encouraged to deliberately postpone important decisions until they have opportunity to gather more information. For example, a counselor might decide to wait until the third counseling session before making a diagnosis.

Finally, counselors should reduce their confidence in a given decision. They should realize that clinical data may be interpreted in more than one way. Faust (1986) notes that few predictive judgments justify extreme confidence. It was pointed out earlier how minority clients may have severe pathology or skillfully use racism as a defense mechanism. Counselors looking at the same clinical data may interpret the client either as being clinically paranoid or a victim of racism. A more accurate interpretation would recognize how the mixture of pathology and victimization are mutually reinforcing. Only competent counselors who form tentative hypotheses, delay decisions, and reduce confidence in their decisions could eventually arrive at this conclusion.

Chapter Summary

Counseling consists of numerous decisions. This chapter described general and personal strategies counselors can employ to improve their decision making. Counselors can broaden their view of assessment, particularize their assessments, contextualize their assessments, use multiple methods of data collection, and interpret test scores cautiously. Counselors can also reduce their personal biases by investigating alternative explanations of behavior, considering probability and base rate data, using confirmatory and disconfirmatory hypothesis testing strategies, and delaying decision making. By following these guidelines, counselors should find themselves making fewer judgmental errors about minority clients. They should also find improvement in their decisions about treatment planning. It is hoped that counselors acquire good habits of decision making as soon as possible.

10

Manage Resistance

An Asian American couple who had serious marital problems once came to me for counseling. The wife was a second-generation Chinese American, whereas the husband had a mixed European and Chinese heritage. During our sessions, the husband made it extremely difficult for us to work together, compounding an already tense situation. He was loud, sarcastic, and intimidating. When questioned about his role in contributing to the problems in their marriage, he shifted the blame to his wife. He accused her of holding on to traditional Chinese values, tried to cut her off when she expressed her feelings, and made excuses for his shortcomings.

The husband was a resistant client. He interfered with progress in counseling. Resistance could very well be the most challenging aspect of counseling. Cavanagh (1982) describes the challenge counselors face in handling resistance:

> Only the most naive counselor would think that being in counseling is an obvious sign that a person is dedicated to change. In reality, most people in counseling have ambivalent feelings toward change, and some people have a vested interest in not changing. Because resistance in counseling is common, it is important for counselors and people in counseling to understand the causes and signs of resistance. This knowledge paves the way for appropriate responses. (p. 240)

Managing the resistance of minority clients is a special challenge, particularly when a counselor and client are not of the same race. Counselors have to work through the special dynamics resulting from racial misunderstanding in addition to the usual dynamics of resistance. Successful resistance management depends primarily upon the ability of counselors to (a) conceptualize resistance and (b) skillfully employ resistance management strategies. This chapter defines resistance, sets forth a typology for classifying client behavior, and describes strategies for resistance management. Examples from multicultural counseling to illustrate these concepts and principles are also provided.

Understanding Resistance

Helping a client change poses an inherent dilemma for most counselors: determining whether or not clients' reactions in counseling serve their own best interest. Not all of a client's change-opposing behavior is resistance, and not all of a client's change-promoting behavior is therapeutic. As a counseling psychologist, I define resistance based upon my extensive experience counseling clients of many backgrounds. *Resistance is countertherapeutic behavior. The behavior is directed toward one goal: the indiscriminate avoidance of the painful requirements of change.*

Here are six principles that can be gleaned from this definition.

1. *Resistance Is Reflected in Behavior.* Like racism, resistance is human motor activity. It can be observed, repeated, and measured. Resistance is not the attitudes or psychological state of the client, although these are powerful motivators of client behavior. Upon observing a client's behavior, counselors might infer the attitudes of the client, but only the client's actual behavior is resistance. Therefore, strategies to manage resistance must aim at behavior first and attitudes second.

2. *Resistance Is Countertherapeutic.* In one way or another, it interferes with counseling. Resistance may slow down counseling, undermine the process, cause premature termination, or set the client up for self-defeat. In whatever form resistance takes, the client always loses out. The ultimate effects of resistance depend upon the degree and type of resistance and how it is managed by the counselor.

3. *Resistance Is Goal-Directed.* It is an attempt to avoid the painful requirements of change. Counseling can be traumatic, much like radical

surgery. The client's avoidance of pain may be explained in terms of costs and benefits. The client may feel that change is more costly than not changing and remaining in the unhealthy state. In the eyes and experience of the client, the cost of changing may outweigh the benefits of changing. Change can be very scary due to the inherent uncertainty it creates.

4. *Resistance Typically Involves Indiscriminate Avoidance of Pain.* In many cases, clients do not evaluate the merits of pain. They avoid any type of pain, whether it is necessary pain related to therapy or unnecessary pain which has no therapeutic value. They may feel the pain of change so intensely that their first and only reaction is to avoid it. But their avoidance comes at a high price: forfeiture of personal growth, healing, and the possibility of having a more fulfilling life.

5. *Resistance Can Take Shape in a Variety of Behaviors.* Any counter-therapeutic behavior, regardless of the shape it takes, is resistance. This means that different clients may use different types of resistance, or one client may employ several types of resistance. Cavanagh (1982) identifies a number of resistant behaviors: canceling appointments or showing up late, evading questions, focusing attention on the counselor, controlling the content of the conversations, or placing the counselor in a dilemma.

6. *Resistance May or May Not Be Observed, Depending Upon Whether the Behavior Occurs in Public or Private.* If resistance is private, counselors must be astute enough to discern its effects, or they are not likely to know it exists. Even perceptive counselors find it hard to detect private resistance, as in the case of a client who withholds important information that could affect diagnosis and treatment planning. Counselors must acknowledge that unobserved resistance, like observed resistance, interferes with counseling.

Client Responses in Counseling

Counselors need a tool to help them classify client behavior either as resistance or nonresistance. A 2 × 2 typology may be such a tool (see Figure 10.1). The typology has two dimensions: client responses to counseling and effects of client responses. Each dimension is further divided into two categories. Client responses to counseling are either change-opposing or change-promoting. When clients oppose change, they try to cling to their

Client Behavior

		Change-Opposing	Change-Promoting
	Countertherapeutic	Antagonism (Resistance)	Acquiescence (Resistance)
Effects of Client Behavior	Therapeutic	Protest (Nonresistance)	Compliance (Nonresistance)

Figure 10.1. Typology for Classifying Client Behavior as Resistant and Nonresistant

old patterns of behavior. When clients promote change, they seek to adopt new patterns of behavior.

The effects of client responses to counseling are either therapeutic or countertherapeutic. Therapeutic effects on clients enhance their personal functioning. In such cases, clients begin to face their problems and relate more realistically to the outside world. Nontherapeutic effects on clients hinder their personal functioning and, in extreme cases, lead to serious psychopathology.

Combinations of the two categories of client responses and effects of client responses yield four possible client response modes: (a) change-opposing behavior contributing to countertherapeutic effects (antagonism), (b) change-promoting behavior contributing to countertherapeutic effects (acquiescence), (c) change-opposing behavior contributing to therapeutic effects (protest), and (d) change-promoting behavior contributing to therapeutic effects (compliance). Each of these client response modes occupies a quadrant of the typology. Client behavior in counseling is either therapeutic or countertherapeutic, meaning that it is nonresistance or resistance. Two quadrants of the typology, antagonism and acquiescence, represent resistance. The other two quadrants, protest and compliance, represent nonresistance.

Most counselors think of resistance as behavior found in quadrant 1, antagonism. Antagonistic clients directly oppose counseling. They often arrive at a premature conclusion about the benefits of counseling, and many of them pay little attention to the merits of the counselor's treatment recommendations. Most resistance probably falls into this category. Examples of antagonism are attacking the counselor, rationalizing the problem, pressing for quick and easy solutions, and dropping out of counseling prematurely.

Another type of resistance is acquiescence. On the surface, acquiescent clients may seem to go along with the counseling. In actuality, they are uncommitted to change and accept uncritically the treatment recommendations of the counselor. An example would be when a counselor asks for feedback on an interpretation of the presenting problem, and the client provides none. An acquiescent client might say "I have no questions about your interpretation. I trust your professional opinion." In this case, the client may have an opinion but quietly resists change by refusing to collaborate with the counselor.

Acquiescence has been overlooked by many counselors as a form of resistance. Perhaps the colloquial meaning of the word resistance, connoting direct force, prevents counselors from seeing more passive client responses as resistance. Nevertheless, acquiescence can be as counter-therapeutic as active forms of resistance.

In quadrant 3, the change-opposing behavior is therapeutic. At first glance, protest may appear to be similar to antagonism, but there is a major difference between these classes of client behavior. Astute counselors understand that protest, unlike antagonism, involves the client's critical evaluation of the counselor's treatment recommendations. Protesting clients have a basic commitment to therapeutic change.

Sometimes clients cooperate with counselors, and their cooperation is therapeutic. This type of client behavior, occupying quadrant 4, is compliance. Compliant clients participate actively in counseling. They are dedicated to personal change and growth. Although change may be painful, they do not allow the painful requirements of change to prevent them from complying with the counselor's recommendations.

The overt behaviors of acquiescence, although appearing to be similar to compliance, are actually different. Acquiescent clients are passive and accept uncritically the counselor's proposals for change. Compliant clients, on the other hand, participate actively in counseling, take ownership of their problems, and accept responsibility for changing. Compliance includes such behaviors as asking clarifying questions, offering the counselor additional insights, following through on homework assignments between sessions, and showing up for appointments punctually and regularly.

Strategies to Manage Resistance

How should counselors handle resistance? They can ignore it. Competent mental health professionals know, however, that resistance will not automatically go away. Ironically, unchallenged resistance is self-perpetuating. The behavior is negatively reinforced by its avoidance of painful demands inherent in change. Counselors have a better option. They can manage resistance, channeling it into an asset rather than looking upon it as a liability. Here are five resistance management strategies available to counselors.

1. Do Not React Defensively to Resistant Clients

Resistant clients may frighten and intimidate counselors. I supervised a psychology intern several years ago who had a very angry client. During one session, the client jumped out of his chair and pounded on the office walls and door. The client's behavior scared the intern, although the intern was not aware of how deeply the experience affected him. As I listened to tapes of subsequent sessions, I noticed that the intern changed his counseling style and became passive. He allowed the client to ramble without probing for much insight or making other therapeutic demands. When I described my observations in supervision and questioned the intern, he began to realize how much he feared the client.

Counselors who react defensively to resistant clients are unaware of their defensiveness and attempts to reduce their emotional pain. To the contrary, they expend considerable effort unconsciously avoiding their uncomfortable feelings. Because of the unrealistic nature of their responses, defensive counselors are not helpful. If anything, their reactions tend to intensify the client's resistance.

Here are examples of counselor defensiveness with resistant minority clients.

- talking excessively about racial issues
- avoiding discussions about racial issues
- making treatment expectations of minority clients unnecessarily easy
- making treatment expectations of minority clients unnecessarily stringent
- using minority expressions and idioms inappropriately to gain acceptance
- emphasizing one's friendship with other members of the client's race
- claiming one's impartiality

- overemphasizing one's support of minority causes
- not examining one's reactions to client resistance
- failing to channel client resistance into an asset rather than a liability

To overcome defensiveness, counselors should anticipate client resistance. Resistance comes in many shapes and forms, and counselors should consider resistance the norm rather than exception in counseling. Then counselors should alert themselves to their uncomfortable feelings. They should try to differentiate feelings triggered by the client from those emanating from other sources. Finally, counselors should identify racial content associated with their feelings. One of the best cues of racial defensiveness is when counselors try to convince themselves that they are not prejudiced.

2. Classify Client Behavior

Counselors should classify client behavior as either resistance or nonresistance. Successful resistance management depends upon this important step. Counselors must thoroughly assess the client's behavior, matching it against the descriptions of the four quadrants of the client behavior typology. In attempting to classify behavior, counselors can make four possible decisions: correctly identifying behavior as resistance, correctly identifying behavior as nonresistance, incorrectly identifying behavior as resistance, and incorrectly identifying behavior as nonresistance.

Two of these decisions are correct, and two are incorrect. One frequent mistake is labeling acquiescence as compliance. Another is labeling protest as antagonism. Counselors must first rule out these types of errors in judgment. Nonresistant behaviors are a sign of a cooperative counseling relationship. These behaviors do not require resistance management. Instead, mental health professionals should encourage compliance.

If counselors initially identify acquiescence or compliance, they must rule out the possibility that one behavior is mistaken for the other. They should note that compliance involves the client's critical examination of the interventions, whereas acquiescence involves passivity and an uncritical acceptance of counseling. Counselors should look for acquiescence in the form of lack of feedback, constructive criticisms, or suggestions from the client. If counselors are still unsure of how to classify the client's behavior, they should directly ask the client for feedback. If the client does not comply, counselors may be reasonably sure that the client is acquiescing.

If counselors believe a client is antagonistic, they must rule out the possibility that the behavior is actually protest. Because the surface behaviors of protest and antagonism may be similar, counselors can distinguish them by thoroughly examining their own interventions for flaws. Of course, counselors cannot always be certain that select interventions are perfectly suited for each client. However, they can attempt to ascertain if client opposition is due to an inappropriate intervention.

Counselors may ask themselves these questions. Do the interventions meet the needs of the minority client? Do I put too much stock in my preferred theoretical orientation? Does my theoretical orientation have implicit cultural bias? Are my expectations of minority clients realistic? Do I expect change too quickly? Answers to these questions should help counselors determine the meaning of the client's change-opposing behavior.

If counseling continues to be problematic, the counselor may be dealing with private antagonism. Counselors cannot observe it, and they have no direct cues except that the client is not making progress. Counselors should become more attentive to the client's homework assignments between sessions and work on strengthening the therapeutic alliance.

3. Confront the Client's Contradictions, Discrepancies, and Inconsistencies

Resistant clients send contradictory messages. This is confusing to counselors who must interpret what clients are actually communicating. A client may claim that he or she wants to benefit from counseling. Yet the client tries to keep the conversation at a surface level. Against this apparent contradiction, the counselor must somehow determine if the client is really interested in counseling.

Interactional counseling is helpful in explaining discrepant behaviors. Watzlawick, Beavin, and Jackson (1967) state that communication occurs on two levels: content and relationship levels. The content level of communication is the factual or semantic meaning of the messages. The relationship level message communicates a message about the content message, and it always accompanies the content message. Haley (1963) states that the relationship message classifies and qualifies the content message. It is metacommunication or communication about communication.

Consider the client who delivers the following content message:

Content Message (compliance implied): I'm used to dealing with White people. I talk to them at work and school. So it doesn't bother me that you are a White counselor.

Then suppose that the client contradicts this content message by sending a different relationship message. When the counselor inquires about intimate details of the client's anxieties, the client consistently skirts the issues and metacommunicates to the counselor:

> **Relationship Message (resistance):**   Don't expect me to spill my guts to you. You're just one more White person who doesn't understand the Black experience.

Many counselors do not perceive the incongruence between content and relationship messages. They are, in effect, oblivious to resistance. If these counselors are to effectively confront resistance, they need to "listen" attentively to the content message, ferret out the relationship message, and attempt to ascertain the degree of congruence between them. Perceptive counselors notice that resistant clients camouflage their relationship messages with content messages. They press these clients to acknowledge the two messages. Then they attempt to get these clients to recognize the inconsistency between the two messages. Finally, they challenge resistant clients to become congruent in communicating subsequent content and relationship messages. In this particular case, counselors might confront the client in the following manner.

> **Counselor:**   On the one hand, you have strongly emphasized your positive relationships with White people outside of counseling. You imply by your comments that race does not make a difference when it comes to being open with people. However, your behavior seems to tell a different story. Every time I encourage you to talk openly about your struggles, you skirt the issues. I'm wondering if the fact that you are so closed really means you don't trust White people and don't care to talk intimately to a White counselor.

4. Expose the Client's Secondary Gains

Some minority clients are skillful manipulators. Even though their behavior is countertherapeutic, they benefit from their actions. Consider minority clients who exploit the situation when White counselors are in need of their approval. They know these counselors need their approval. So they play games and put the counselors on the defensive. If one recognizes that minorities are victims of racism, it is easy to understand how clients would find it exhilarating to exploit the power differential with a professional. The purpose of gaming is to put themselves in a psychological one-up position. This is a tremendous benefit to minority clients whose usual experience is the one-down position.

Many counselors are oblivious to the gaming. Others sense it but do not know what to do about it. The best approach for counselors is to remain alert to signs of manipulation and then directly expose it. A White teacher described how she handled a couple of Black female students. When she realized what was happening, she said, "You're playing a game with me." The girls laughed, indicating that they knew the teacher had caught on to them. Once the gaming is exposed, it is difficult to continue to use it as a manipulative strategy.

Exposing the client's secondary gains is not the only responsibility of counselors. They should take the lead in discussing the purpose served by gaming. Minority clients need to come to terms with the necessity of these games in the first place. Consider this counselor intervention.

> **Counselor:** You seemed to take great delight in using rap rhetoric which you knew I didn't understand. It was real important to you that I did not know where you were coming from. I think this is one of the reasons we are not making much progress now. What do you get out of playing games with me? Why do you feel so good in trying to fool me? We need to talk about this.

5. Reframe the Client's Definition of Control

Many clients are afraid of counseling. They may fear the pain of growth, starting new behaviors, stopping old behaviors, or disclosing intimate details of their lives to another person. To deal with their insecurities, they try to control the counselor and the counseling situation. Counselors can disarm this type of resistance by giving clients a new definition of control.

First, they should empathize with their clients' fears. In this way, counselors help clients accept the fact that their feelings are legitimate. The last thing counselors should do is overlook, minimize, or invalidate the feelings of their clients. Competent counselors know that clients typically act out their unacknowledged fears in the form of self-defeating behaviors. Here are two empathic interventions counselors can make.

> **Counselor A:** It's not uncommon for people to have apprehensions about changing their lives. It can be really scary.
>
> **Counselor B:** Your reluctance to talk to a White counselor is perfectly understandable. You don't want to put yourself in another position to discuss your feelings with one more White person who thinks he understands when he really doesn't.

Second, counselors should tell resistant clients that their resistance is a form of control. They should explain how the client's fear-motivated actions are countertherapeutic. Counselors can point out the short-term benefits of these control strategies, but they should also explain how their control strategies are costly. Counselors can use this discussion to suggest constructive strategies for the client to adopt. This comment illustrates a helpful intervention.

> **Counselor:** There are real benefits for you in trying to put me on the defensive. You might succeed in getting me to back off. And, if you do, you might not have to look at yourself. But this could be costly to you. You may pass up an opportunity to learn how to handle your problems. Let me suggest you give up trying to control our conversation and put that same energy into speaking up for yourself when people try to take advantage of you.

Third, counselors should encourage clients to talk openly about their fears and insecurities. Counselors can help clients understand that feelings, even so-called negative ones, serve a useful purpose. Counselors can then help clients connect their feelings with personal problem-solving strategies.

> **Counselor:** Tell me about your experiences of being misunderstood by White people. I want to hear your side of the story. I also want to be the type of person who helps you put your feelings into perspective and find workable solutions to your problems.

6. Confront Normative Resistance

Some resistance reflects the norms of the client's culture rather than individual idiosyncracies. Counselors can trace the resistance back to values embedded in the culture. Anyone from the client's culture would likely show this type of resistance. Many Asian clients, for instance, save face by not discussing family problems. They do not want to bring shame upon themselves or their families by admitting they have psychological problems. Counselors who ignore this cultural norm probably create a bigger problem than they solve.

To confront normative resistance, counselors should begin by recognizing the anxiety-reducing function of cultural norms. They can discover important cultural values by observing and listening to a client's reactions to proposals for change. Then counselors should avoid imposing their values on the client. Eventually, counselors may need to challenge normative resistance when it is obviously countertherapeutic. In so doing, counselors must also show support and respect for the client's cultural traditions. Here is a confrontation of normative resistance.

> **Counselor:** Like many people from your culture, you do not want to bring shame upon your family. That is a long-standing tradition and one that is important to you. I want you, however, to reevaluate your unwillingness to talk about family matters. You have a lot of feelings bottled up inside you, and you continue to feel very depressed. This is one time I think you should consider how your tradition is hurting you rather than helping you.

Chapter Summary

Unmanaged resistance in multicultural counseling can lead to unintentional racism. Many counselors, skilled in diagnosis and intervention planning, are equally unskilled in handling resistance, especially with minority clients. This chapter defined resistance, provided a behavior typology for classifying client behavior, and described six resistance management strategies. Counselors who adopt these strategies should find themselves better able to facilitate therapeutic change with minority clients, for some of whom constructive change is not a priority.

11

Terminate Effectively

Every counseling relationship must come to an end. The type of ending—like every other phase of counseling—is critical to the success of counseling. Cormier and Hackney (1993) suggest that termination is not just a significant moment in the counseling relationship; it is an essential part of the therapeutic process. Ideally, the conclusion of counseling should be timely, occurring only after the chosen outcome goals have been reached. But reaching important goals is not the ultimate test of effective termination. The real test lies in maintaining therapeutic gains long after counseling is over.

Effective termination contributes to the client's personal growth and development. Ineffective termination, by contrast, can jeopardize counseling, even a counseling relationship that is otherwise successful. Because minority consumers often have poor outcomes, express dissatisfaction with counseling and drop out prematurely, effective termination is a necessity in multicultural counseling. But effective termination does not happen automatically. It requires a plan of action.

Teyber (1992) clearly describes why a conscientious plan of termination is necessary:

> Termination is an important and distinct phase of therapy that must be negotiated thoughtfully. Ending the therapeutic relationship will almost

always be of great significance to clients. The way in which this separation experience is resolved is so important that it influences how well clients will be able to resolve future conflicts in their lives. More specifically, the way in which the termination is dealt with helps determine whether clients leave therapy with a greater sense of their own personal resources and ability to manage their own lives. . . . Therapists must be prepared to utilize the potential for change that is still available as therapists and clients prepare to end their relationship. (p. 246)

This chapter examines termination in counseling. According to Gladding (1992), termination is a multidimensional process. With this in mind, this chapter looks at how to counteract unintentional racism when terminating with minority clients. What follows is a description of a variety of constructive termination-related procedures.

Reduce the Chances of Premature Termination

Wierzbicki and Pekarik (1993) conducted a meta-analysis of 125 studies of psychotherapy dropout. They found that dropout was significantly related to racial minority status. Specifically, minority clients show a higher rate of premature termination than nonminority clients. Although it is impossible to know all of the factors that contribute to this outcome, there are two likely sources. Both relate to process goals.

First, many counselors fail to establish a strong therapeutic alliance with minority clients. The consequences of this failure cannot be overemphasized. What some counselors do not realize is the amount of anxiety and intimidation the client feels. Add to this the counselor's insensitivity, and client dropout seems inevitable. The case of Nor Shala described in Chapter 8 clearly illustrates this point.

Consider one of my counseling cases that turned out to be a failure. A young Black woman was referred to me for counseling. In every sense of the word, the client was clinically paranoid. She felt extremely vulnerable and did not allow people to get to know her. Almost from the outset of our first session, I began to strongly confront her. I wanted to break through her defenses. By taking this approach, however, I violated one of my own therapeutic principles: establish a therapeutic alliance before confronting a client. Instead, I acted out of frustration and impatience. This proved to be a fatal mistake. The more I pressed her to open up, the more she withdrew. After three sessions, the young woman terminated. We did not make progress. Perhaps, I even discouraged her from ever returning to see a counselor.

Second, counselors should clarify for minority clients the nature of counseling. Many minorities are either unfamiliar with how counseling works or have different expectations than counselors about the process. Dauphinais et al. (1981) found that counselors committed to client-centered or nondirective methods were ineffective with Native American adolescents. The adolescents did not understand the good intentions of the counselors. Instead, they thought the counselors were being evasive. The counselors probably assumed the adolescents were being resistant. This example demonstrates the need for counselors to minimize any confusion minority clients may have about counseling. It also illustrates why counselors have to adjust their counseling styles if they are to be culturally responsive. Finally, it shows why counselors must clearly communicate with minority clients.

Conclude Each Session Effectively

One way to prevent premature dropout is to conclude each counseling session effectively. Counselors should conclude each session with a summary of the major themes and accomplishments of counseling up to that point. They should reinforce clients for their accomplishments and therapeutic work. As much as possible, counselors should encourage clients to return for the next session. If counselors remind themselves of the pain involved in dealing with personal issues as well as the ongoing challenges minorities face outside of counseling, they could see how these clients might get discouraged and drop out. Effective session termination can counteract such discouragement.

There are several additional ways counselors can try to make the conclusion of counseling sessions effective.

Clearly Define Time Limits (Hackney & Cormier, 1988; Pietrofesa, Hoffman, & Splete, 1984). Scissons (1993) suggests that the conclusion of a session should not be a surprise. He gives an example of what a counselor might say.

Counselor: Cornelius, we will have one hour together this morning. Let's start by . . . (p. 178)

Establishing time parameters is especially important in working with minority clients. Their expectations and cultural values may clash with those of the counselor. Unless these differences are clarified, clients may be surprised by the time limits imposed by the counselor.

Do Not Begin New Topics Near the Ending of a Session (Benjamin, 1981; Scissons, 1993). If the client introduces new material, show empathic understanding, but try to postpone discussion of the topic to the next session. Scissons (1993) gives a useful example.

> **Counselor:** Maxine, I sense that the matter of your relationship with your father is an important one. I doubt that we will be able to deal with it adequately today because we have only about five minutes left. Perhaps next week we should devote as much time as we need to talk about your relationship with your father. In the meantime, why don't you think about what you will want to talk about next week. (pp. 178-179)

Because many minority clients are mistrustful of the counseling process, counselors must carefully handle information introduced late in the session. They need to show clients that their concerns are taken seriously. They cannot afford to turn off minority clients. At the same time, they should be professional and keep their appointments on schedule.

Build a Bridge Between Sessions. A frequent flaw in counseling is the lack of connectedness and continuity between sessions. To overcome this problem, counselors should (a) summarize the progress made thus far, (b) outline future directions, and (c) assign homework between sessions. Homework assignments are useful in helping clients test out their accomplishments and implement lifestyle changes. They also serve as a link to the next session where the counselor can review the client's progress. Scissons (1993) gives an example of a transitioning intervention.

> **Counselor:** Jardine, there are several things you can do during the week we are apart that will help us in our time together next week. Perhaps the most helpful thing would be . . . (p. 179)

Recycle or Refer When Appropriate

Sometimes counseling reaches an impasse, and the impasse might not be the result of client resistance. Other factors involving the counselor or counseling setting may contribute to the impasse. When this occurs, counselors must change their strategy. Two alternative strategies are recycling and referral.

Recycling involves a reexamination of all phases of the therapeutic process (Baruth & Huber, 1985). After a period of time, counselors should look back over their work with a client. They should try to determine the strengths and weaknesses of their counseling. Then they should try to determine where improvements are needed. Because counseling is a human endeavor, some well-intentioned efforts of counselors may not succeed. Thus recycling is an opportunity to review, reevaluate, revise, and reinvest in counseling.

A number of factors may cause an impasse in counseling. Some of these are:

- inadequate problem definition
- inappropriate or poorly implemented interventions
- miscommunication of expectations between counselor and client
- judgmental and inferential errors
- incompatible personalities
- counselor's misunderstanding of cultural dynamics

Chapter 4 described the expert role that many counselors take on. Reflecting their medical model orientation, counselors who play expert are prone to attribute therapeutic failure to minority clients. It is rare for counselors to look at themselves as the cause of failure. If, after recycling, counseling is still not successful, counselors should take an honest look at themselves. They should have the courage and humility to acknowledge their limitations. If they determine that they cannot help a client, they should make a referral.

Okun (1992) states that a referral involves arranging other assistance for a client when the initial arrangement is not helpful. Counselors who cannot relate to minority clients or who are incompetent to treat them should make a referral. Several authors have argued that it is unethical to treat minority clients without the appropriate training (Fields, 1979; Korman, 1974). I have argued that this could be a violation of a minority client's civil rights (Ridley, 1985a).

Gladding (1992) recognizes the importance of timing in making referrals:

> If a counselor suspects an impasse with a certain client, the counselor should
> refer that client as soon as possible. On the other hand, if the counselor has

worked with the client for a while, the counselor should be sensitive in giving the client enough time to get used to the idea of working with someone else. (p. 239)

To make helpful referrals, counselors should become familiar with referral resources and match the client with the best possible referral (Baruth & Huber, 1985). For minority clients, this means counselors should be aware of referral sources that are responsive to multicultural issues.

Evaluate Counseling Outcomes

Evaluating and monitoring counseling goals is the only way to tell if counseling is successful. Counselors cannot be certain if they are benefitting minority clients unless they have a system for tracking progress. Otherwise, they can only guess about the benefits of counseling. Baruth and Huber (1985) suggest five commonly used measures to evaluate counseling outcomes. These should be helpful in determining the extent to which therapeutic goals are achieved with minority clients.

Verbal Self-Report. Baruth and Huber (1985) state that this is the easiest and most convenient type of evaluation. Self-reports are direct sources of data. They come directly from the client. Although they are easy to use and convenient, self-reports tend not to have high reliability. Many clients tend to give socially desirable responses. Cormier and Cormier (1991) state that self-reports are often used in conjunction with other outcome measures that produce more concrete and quantifiable data.

Frequency Counts. This type of measurement reflects the number of times a specific aspect of client functioning occurs. The functioning may be an emotional state, thought, or behavior. Counting the number of anxiety attacks, self-denigrating thoughts, or inappropriate behaviors within a particular time frame illustrates this form of measurement.

Duration Counts. Baruth and Huber (1985) define this type of evaluation as the length of time a response or collection of responses occurs. These authors give the examples of the amount of time spent speaking, length of depressive thoughts, and length of anxiety attacks.

There are two ways of obtaining frequency counts and duration counts: continuous recording and time sampling. In continuous recording, client responses are recorded each time the specific response occurs. In time sampling, clients track selected responses during specific time intervals. Time sampling is not as precise as continuous recording, but it is more practical.

Rating Scales. Rating scales assess the intensity or degree of specific responses. Baruth and Huber (1985) give the example of anxiety, which can be measured using a rating scale of 1 (calm) to 5 (panic-stricken). Cronback (1970) offers several criteria for using rating scales. These include well-defined responses, descriptions for each point on a rating scale, and at least four and no more than seven graduations.

Checklists. Checklists are used to determine the presence or absence of a particular response. These require counselors to use a different type of judgment from rating scales, which assess degree or intensity. Baruth and Huber (1985) suggest the use of checklists with clients who seek to be more assertive. The client's assertive behaviors can be observed and recorded on a checklist.

Recommend Alternative Modalities

In addition to providing individual counseling and therapy, counselors may recommend other treatment modalities. Tharp (1991) describes a number of modalities that have been used with culturally diverse clients. To varying degrees, these modalities include family and community members and settings. His list includes group therapy, problem solving and social skills training, family therapy, home-based treatment, network treatment, and community interventions. Tharp gives examples of the application of these modalities to minority populations.

Counselors can employ these modalities in several ways. For some clients, one of these interventions may be used to replace individual therapy as the treatment of choice. For some clients, one or more of these modalities may be used to complement individual therapy. As an example, a Native American may be seen in weekly sessions, while the counselor networks to solve shared problems among the clan. Certainly, the counselor should use discretion and show sensitivity to ethical issues such as confidentiality. For still other clients, alternative modalities can be employed once the client terminates individual therapy. After a client gains insight into some personal issues, family therapy or home-based treatment may be logical sequels to individual therapy.

Follow Up When Counseling Is Over

It may be helpful to minority clients if counselors show continued interest in them after termination. Counselors can show interest by checking up on clients to determine their progress. According to Okun (1992), many counselors do not follow up on clients. They probably believe that their responsibilities to clients are over once counseling formally terminates.

It is understandable why counselors do not follow up. They have busy schedules, heavy caseloads, and the need to make billable hours. In some cases, service agencies restrict the number of client contact hours by requiring time-limited therapy. Despite these pressures, Young (1992) reminds counselors that follow-up contacts offer opportunities for clients to return to therapy if necessary. These contacts provide a source of additional encouragement even if the client does not return. In minority communities, where mental health agencies are often looked upon with suspicion, follow-up on clients is a way to create a positive image.

During the final counseling session, counselors should reassure clients that they can return. By leaving the door open, clients can feel free to deal with old problems that flare up or new problems that develop. Here are several follow-up strategies.

- Write a personalized letter, showing interest in the client's progress.
- Make a phone call to the client, showing interest in the client's progress.
- Send the client self-help materials.
- Invite the client to relevant workshops or seminars.
- Inform the client of new treatment services that might be beneficial.

Prevent Relapse

Changing problem behavior is one accomplishment. Maintaining constructive change is another. The real test of effective termination lies in maintaining therapeutic gains long after counseling is over. Competent counselors should attempt to help minority clients prevent relapse of problem behaviors.

Marlatt (1982) developed a model to understand the relapse process. The model is used to understand addictive disorders such as alcoholism, smoking, and obesity. Watson and Tharp (1993), however, note that the model applies to any self-change effort in which there is danger of a client falling back into problem behaviors. This includes problems with gambling, exercising, studying, depression, unwanted sexual behavior, procrastination, and many others.

As a counselor, you can help minority clients prevent relapse by taking the following steps.

1. *Identify High-Risk Situations.* High-risk situations are those in which the client's problem behavior is most likely to occur. High-risk situations vary from person to person. What may be a high-risk situation for one client may be low-risk for another.

Counselors can assist clients in mapping out the relationship between problem behaviors and the context in which they occur. They can also help them identify low-risk situations in which their problem behaviors are less likely to occur. Counselors should help clients avoid high-risk situations and maximize time spent in low-risk situations.

2. *Develop Coping Skills for High-Risk Situations.* High-risk situations are not always avoidable (Watson & Tharp, 1993). Consequently, clients need to learn how to successfully handle risky situations when they arise. Marlatt and Gordon (1985) propose several problem-solving skills to deal with high-risk situations.

- List the details of the problem.
- Think of as many solutions to the problem as possible.
- Select solutions to use.
- Check to ensure you actually implement the solutions.

3. *Prevent Lapses From Becoming Relapses.* A lapse is a single event or reemergence of a previous problem behavior. It may or may not lead to a state of relapse (Brownell, Marlatt, Lichtenstein, & Wilson, 1986). A lapse does not mean the client is a total failure. Clients need to know this and use a lapse as an opportunity to learn from their mistakes and make steady improvement.

Watson and Tharp (1993) suggest that clients need a plan to deal with lapses; they must put on the brakes before they totally relapse. The plan should consist of self-monitoring of the problem behavior, a self-contract for what to do in the event of a lapse, and a reminder card that puts the lapse into proper perspective and encourages the client.

4. *Develop Social Support.* Social support is one of the most important factors associated with successful relapse prevention. Before therapy terminates, counselors can assist minority clients in developing and cultivating their social support networks. There are a variety of avenues counselors can take. They can train family and friends in how to play a supportive role. Counselors can help clients get involved in community services and support groups. Counselors can also work with clients to get support from churches in their community or other natural support systems. Again, the alternative modalities described by Tharp (1991) can be used to develop social support.

Chapter Summary

Termination of counseling is inevitable. Competent counselors use this culminating phase of counseling to advance the goals set for clients. Counselors can reduce the chance of premature termination, conclude each session effectively, recycle or refer when appropriate, evaluate counseling outcomes, recommend alternative modalities, follow up when counseling is over, and engage in relapse prevention. By employing these termination-related procedures, counselors can help minority clients to maximize the gains made during the course of counseling.

References

Adams, P. L. (1970). Dealing with racism in biracial psychiatry. *Journal of the American Academy of Child Psychiatry, 9*(1), 33-43.

Adams, W. A. (1950). The Negro patient in psychiatric treatment. *American Journal of Orthopsychiatry, 20*(2), 305-310.

Adebimpe, V. R. (1981). Overview: White norms and psychiatric diagnosis of black patients. *American Journal of Psychiatry, 138*(3), 279-285.

Adebimpe, V. R. (1982). Psychiatric symptoms in black patients. In S. M. Turner & R. T. Jones (Eds.), *Behavior modification in black populations: Psychosocial issues and empirical findings* (pp. 57-71). New York: Plenum.

Allport, G. W. (1946). Personalistic psychology as a science: A reply. *Psychological Review, 53,* 132-135.

American Counseling Association. (1988). *Ethical standards* (rev. ed.). Alexandria, VA: Author.

American Psychiatric Association. (1994). *Diagnostic and statistical manual of mental disorders* (4th ed.). Washington, DC: Author.

American Psychological Association. (1992). Ethical principles of psychologists and code of conduct. *American Psychologist, 47*(12), 1597-1611.

Anastasi, A. (1992). What counselors should know about the use and interpretation of psychological tests. *Journal of Counseling and Development, 70*(5), 610-615.

Anderson, L. P. (1991). Acculturative stress: A theory of relevance to black Americans. *Clinical Psychology Review, 11*(6), 685-702.

Arax, M. (1987, April 12). Clash of two worlds leaves many in pain. *Los Angeles Times.*

Aristotle. (1952). *Metaphysics* (Richard Hope, Trans.). New York: Columbia University Press.

Arkes, H. R. (1981). Impediments to accurate clinical judgment and possible ways to minimize their impact. *Journal of Consulting and Clinical Psychology, 49*(3), 323-330.

Atkinson, D. R., Maruyama, M., & Matsui, S. (1978). Effects of counselor race and counseling approach on Asian Americans' perceptions of counselor credibility and utility. *Journal of Counseling Psychology, 25*(1), 76-83.

Atkinson, D. R., & Matsushita, Y. J. (1991). Japanese-American acculturation, counseling style, counselor ethnicity, and perceived counselor credibility. *Journal of Counseling Psychology, 38*(4), 473-478.

Atkinson, D. R., Morten, G., & Sue, D. W. (Eds.). (1993). *Counseling American minorities: A cross-cultural perspective* (4th ed.). Madison, WI: W. C. Brown & Benchmark.

Atkinson, D. R., Thompson, C. E., & Grant, S. K. (1993). A three-dimensional model for counseling racial/ethnic minorities. *The Counseling Psychologist, 21*(2), 257-277.

Axelson, J. A. (1993). *Counseling and development in a multicultural society* (2nd ed.). Pacific Grove, CA: Brooks/Cole.

Bartlett, F. C. (1932). *Remembering: A study in experimental and social psychology.* Cambridge: Cambridge University Press.

Baruth, L. G., & Huber, C. H. (1985). *Counseling and psychotherapy: Theoretical analyses and skills applications.* Columbus, Ohio: Charles E. Merrill.

Batson, C. D., Jones, C. H., & Cochran, P. J. (1979). Attributional bias in counselors' diagnoses: The effects of resources. *Journal of Applied Social Psychology, 9*(4), 377-393.

Belkin, G. S. (1984). *Introduction to counseling* (2nd ed.). Dubuque, IA: William C. Brown.

Bemporad, J. R., Smith, H. F., Hanson, G., & Cicchetti, D. (1982). Borderline syndromes in childhood: Criteria for diagnosis. *American Journal of Psychiatry, 139*(5), 596-602.

Benjamin, A. (1981). *The helping interview* (3rd ed.). Boston: Houghton Mifflin.

Bernard, V. W. (1953). Psychoanalysis and members of minority groups. *Journal of the American Psychoanalytic Association, 1*(2), 256-267.

Beverly, C. (1989). Treatment issues for black, alcoholic clients. *Social Casework: The Journal of Contemporary Social Work, 70*(6), 370-374.

Bieri, J., Lobeck, R., & Galinsky, M. D. (1959). A comparison of direct, indirect, and fantasy measures of identification. *Journal of Abnormal and Social Psychology, 58,* 253-258.

Block, C. B. (1981). Black Americans and the cross-cultural counseling and psychotherapy experience. In A. J. Marsella & P. B. Pedersen (Eds.), *Cross-cultural counseling and psychotherapy* (pp. 177-194). New York: Pergamon.

Bloombaum, M., Yamamoto, J., & James, Q. (1968). Cultural stereotyping among psychotherapists. *Journal of Consulting and Clinical Psychology, 32*(1), 99.

Boyd-Franklin, N. (1989). *Black families in therapy: A multisystems approach.* New York: Guilford.

Brantley, T. (1983). Racism and its impact on psychotherapy. *American Journal of Psychiatry, 140*(12), 1605-1608.

Bronstein, P. A., & Quina, K. (Eds.). (1988). *Teaching a psychology of people: Resources for gender and sociocultural awareness.* Washington, DC: American Psychological Association.

Brown, R. (1965). *Social psychology.* New York: Free Press.

Brownell, K. D., Marlatt, G. A., Lichtenstein, E., & Wilson, G. T. (1986). Understanding and preventing relapse. *American Psychologist, 41*(7), 765-782.

Butts, H. F. (1971). Psychoanalysis and unconscious racism. *Journal of Contemporary Psychotherapy, 3*(2), 67-81.

Calnek, M. (1970). Racial factors in the counter-transference: The black therapist and the black client. *American Journal of Orthopsychiatry, 40*(1), 39-46.

Carter, J. H. (1979). Frequent mistakes made with black patients in psychotherapy. *Journal of the National Medical Association, 71*(10), 1007-1009.

Carter, J. H. (1983). Sociocultural factors in the psychiatric assessment of black patients: A case study. *Journal of the National Medical Association, 75*(8), 817-820.

Casas, J. M. (1984). Policy, training, and research in counseling psychology: The racial/ ethnic minority perspective. In S. D. Brown & R. W. Lent (Eds.), *Handbook of counseling psychology* (pp. 785-831). New York: John Wiley.

Casimir, G. J., & Morrison, B. J. (1993). Rethinking work with "Multicultural Populations." *Community Mental Health Journal, 29*(6), 547-559.

Cavanagh, M. E. (1982). *The counseling experience: A theoretical and practical approach.* Pacific Grove, CA: Brooks/Cole.

Centers for Disease Control. (1992, January). *HIV/AIDS surveillance report* (1-22). Atlanta, GA: Author.

Chess, S., Clark, K. B., & Thomas, A. (1953). The importance of cultural evaluation in psychiatric diagnosis and treatment. *Psychiatric Quarterly, 27*(1), 102-114.

Christoff, K. A., & Kelly, J. A. (1985). A behavioral approach to social skills training with psychiatric patients. In L. L'Abate & M. A. Milan (Eds.), *Handbook of social skills training and research* (pp. 361-387). New York: John Wiley.

Clark, A. J. (1991). The identification and modification of defense mechanisms in counseling. *Journal of Counseling and Development, 69*(3), 231-236.

Committee for Economic Development. (1987). *Children in need: Investment strategies for the educationally disadvantaged: A statement.* New York: Author.

Cook, D. A., & Helms, J. E. (1988). Visible racial/ethnic group supervisees' satisfaction with cross-cultural supervision as predicted by relationship characteristics. *Journal of Counseling Psychology, 35*(3), 268-274.

Coonerty, S. M. (1991). Change in the change agents growth in the capacity to heal. In R. C. Curtis & G. Stricker (Eds.), *How people change: Inside and outside therapy* (pp. 81-97). New York: Plenum.

Cooper, S. (1973). A look at the effect of racism on clinical work. *Social Casework, 54*(2), 76-84.

Corey, G. (1991). *Theory and practice of counseling and psychotherapy* (4th ed.). Pacific Grove, CA: Brooks/Cole.

Corey, G., Corey, M. S., Callanan, P. (1993). *Issues and ethics in the helping professions* (4th ed.). Pacific Grove, CA: Brooks/Cole.

Cormier, L. S., & Hackney, H. (1993). *The professional counselor: A process guide to helping* (2nd ed.). Boston: Allyn & Bacon.

Cormier, W. H., & Cormier, L. S. (1991). *Interviewing strategies for helpers: Fundmental skills and behavioral interventions* (3rd ed.). Pacific Grove, CA: Brooks/Cole.

Corvin, S. A., & Wiggins, F. (1989). An antiracism training model for white professionals. *Journal of Multicultural Counseling and Development, 17*(3), 105-114.

Cronback, L. J. (1970). *Essentials of psychological testing* (3rd ed.). New York: Harper & Row.

Dana, R. H. (1993). *Multicultural assessment perspectives for professional psychology.* Boston: Allyn & Bacon.

d'Ardenne, P. (1993). Transcultural counseling and psychotherapy in the 1990s. *British Journal of Guidance and Counseling, 21*(1), 1-7.

Darwin, C. (1959). *On the origin of species by means of natural selection.* London: J. Murray.

Dauphinais, P., Dauphinais, L., & Rowe, W. (1981). Effects of race and communication style on Indian perceptions of counselor effectiveness. *Counselor Education and Supervision, 21*(1), 72-80.

Davis, F. J. (1978). *Minority-dominant relations: A sociological analysis.* Arlington Heights, IL: AHM.

de Anda, D. (1984). Bicultural socialization: Factors affecting the minority experience. *Social Work, 29*(2), 101-107.

deGobineau, A. (1915). *The inequality of human races.* New York: Putman.

Dixon, V. (1971). Two approaches to black-white relations. In V. Dixon & B. Foster (Eds.), *Beyond black or white? An alternative America* (pp. 23-66). Boston: Little, Brown.

Dovidio, J. F., & Gaertner, S. L. (Eds.). (1986). *Prejudice, discrimination, and racism.* Orlando, FL: Academic Press.

Draguns, J. G. (1989). Dilemmas and choices in cross-cultural counseling: The universal versus the culturally distinctive. In P. B. Pedersen, J. G. Draguns, W. J. Lonner, & J. E. Trimble (Eds.), *Counseling across cultures* (3rd ed.) (pp. 3-21). Honolulu: University of Hawaii Press.

Dreger, R. M., & Miller, K. S. (1960). Comparative psychological studies of Negroes and whites in the United States. *Psychological Bulletin, 57*(5), 361-402.

DuBois, W. E. B. (1969). *The souls of black folk.* New York: New American Library.

Dumont, F., & Lecomte, C. (1987). Inferential processes in clinical work: Inquiry into logical errors that affect diagnostic judgments. *Professional Psychology: Research and Practice, 18*(5), 433-438.

Edwards, A. W. (1982). The consequences of error in selecting treatment for blacks. *Social Casework: The Journal of Contemporary Social Work, 63*(7), 429-433.

Egan, G. (1994). *The skilled helper: A problem-management approach to helping* (5th ed.). Pacific Grove, CA: Brooks/Cole.

Einhorn, H. J., & Hogarth, R. M. (1978). Confidence in judgment: Persistence of the illusion of validity. *Psychological Review, 85*(5), 395-416.

Eisenberg, L. (1962). If not now, when? *American Journal of Orthopsychiatry, 32*(5), 781-793.

Engel, G. L. (1977). The need for a new medical model: A challenge for biomedicine. *Science, 196*(4286), 129-136.

Espin, O. M. (1985). Psychotherapy with Hispanic women: Some considerations. In P. Pedersen (Ed.), *Handbook of cross-cultural counseling and therapy* (pp. 165-171). Westport, CT: Greenwood Press.

Everett, F., Proctor, N., & Cartmell, B. (1983). Providing psychological services to American Indian children and families. *Professional Psychology: Research and Practice, 14*(5), 588-603.

Fairchild, H. H. (1991). Scientific racism: The cloak of objectivity. *Journal of Social Issues, 47*(3), 101-115.

Faust, D. (1986). Research on human judgment and its application to clinical practice. *Professional Psychology: Research and Practice, 17*(5), 420-430.

Fernando, S. (1988). *Race and culture in psychiatry.* London: Croom Helm.

Fields, S. (1979). Mental health and the melting pot. *Innovations, 6*(2), 2-3.

Finkelhor, D. (1984). *Child sexual abuse: New theory and research.* New York: Free Press.

Flaherty, J., & Meagher, R. (1980). Measuring racial bias in inpatient treatment. *American Journal of Psychiatry, 137*(6), 679-682.

Freud, S. (1949). *An outline of psychoanalysis* (J. Strachey, Trans.). New York: Norton.

Freud, S. (1989). *Inhibitions, symptoms, and anxiety.* New York: Norton. (Original work published 1926)

Freud, S. (1963). The dynamics of transference (J. Riviere, Trans.). In P. Rieff (Ed.), *Freud: Therapy and technique.* New York: Collier. (Original work published 1912)

Galton, F. (1869). *Hereditary genius: An inquiry into its laws and consequences.* London: Macmillan.

Gambrill, E. (1990). *Critical thinking in clinical practice: Improving the accuracy of judgments and decisions about clients.* San Francisco: Jossey-Bass.

Gardner, L. H. (1971). The therapeutic relationship under varying conditions of race. *Psychotherapy: Theory, Research and Practice, 8*(1), 78-87.

Garretson, D. J. (1993). Psychological misdiagnosis of African Americans. *Journal of Multicultural Counseling and Development, 21*(2), 119-126.

Garza, A. (1981). Potential pitfalls in the diagnosis and treatment of minority groups. *Journal of Social Psychology, 114,* 9-22.

Geller, J. D. (1988). Racial bias in the evaluation of patients for psychotherapy. In L. Comas-Díaz & E. H. Griffith (Eds.), *Clinical guidelines in cross-cultural mental health* (pp. 112-134). New York: John Wiley.

Gelso, C. J., & Carter, J. A. (1985). The relationship in counseling and psychotherapy: Components, consequences, and theoretical antecedents. *The Counseling Psychologist, 13*(2), 155-243.

Gelso, C. J., & Fretz, B. R. (1992). *Counseling psychology.* Fort Worth, TX: Harcourt Brace Jovanovich.

Gerrard, N. (1991). Racism and sexism, together, in counselling: Three women of colour tell their stories. *Canadian Journal of Counselling, 25*(4), 555-566.

Gladding, S. T. (1992). *Counseling: A comprehensive profession* (2nd ed.). New York: Merrill.

Goffman, E. (1961). *Asylums: Essays on the social situation of mental patients and other inmates.* Chicago: Aldine.

Gold, M. S., & Pearsall, H. R. (1983). Hypothyroidism—or is it depression? *Psychosomatics, 24*(7), 646-651, 654-656.

Goldstein, M. J., Baker, B. L., & Jamison, K. R. (1986). *Abnormal psychology* (2nd ed.). Boston: Little, Brown.

Gomez, E. A., Ruiz, P., & Laval, R. (1982). Psychotherapy and bilingualism: Is acculturation important? *Journal of Operational Psychiatry, 13*(1), 13-16.

Gong-Guy, E., Cravens, R. B., & Patterson, T. E. (1991). Clinical issues in mental health service delivery to refugees. *American Psychologist, 46*(6), 642-648.

Goodman, J. A. (Ed.). (1973). *Dynamics of racism in social work practice.* Washington, DC: National Association of Social Workers.

Grantham, R. J. (1973). Effects of counselor sex, race, and language style on black students in initial interviews. *Journal of Counseling Psychology, 20*(6), 553-559.

Greene, B. (1994). Ethnic-minority lesbians and gay men: Mental health and treatment issues. *Journal of Consulting and Clinical Psychology, 62*(2), 243-251.

Grier, W. H., & Cobbs, P. M. (1968). *Black rage.* New York: Basic Books.

Grier, W. H., & Cobbs, P. M. (1992). *Black rage* (2nd ed.). New York: Basic Books.

Griffin, J. (1961). *Black like me.* Boston: Houghton Mifflin.

Griffith, M. S. (1977). The influences of race on the psychotherapeutic relationship. *Psychiatry, 40*(1), 27-40.

Griffith, M. S., & Jones, E. E. (1978). Race and psychotherapy: Changing perspectives. In J. H. Masserman (Ed.), *Current psychiatric therapies* (Vol. 18, pp. 225-235). New York: Grune & Stratton.

Gross, H., Herbert, M. R., Knotterud, G. L., & Donner, L. (1969). The effect of race and sex on the variation of diagnosis and disposition in a psychiatric emergency room. *Journal of Nervous Mental Disease, 148*(6), 638-642.

Guthrie, R. V. (1976). *Even the rat was white: A historical view of psychology.* New York: Harper & Row.

Hackney, H., & Cormier, L. S. (1988). *Counseling strategies and interventions* (3rd ed.). Englewood Cliffs, NJ: Prentice Hall.

Haettenschwiller, D. L. (1971). Counseling black college students in special programs. *Personnel and Guidance Journal, 50*(1), 29-35.

Haley, J. (1963). *Strategies of psychotherapy.* New York: Grune & Stratton.

Hall, E. T. (1973). *The silent language.* Garden City, NY: Anchor Press/Doubleday.

Hall, G. S. (1904). *Adolescence: Its psychology and its relations to physiology, anthropology, sociology, sex, crime, religion, and education: Vol. 2.* New York: D. Appleton.

Halleck, S. L. (1971, April). Therapy is the handmaiden of the status quo. *Psychology Today,* pp. 30-34, 98-100.

Harrison, D. K. (1975). Race as a counselor-client variable in counseling and psychotherapy: A review of the research. *The Counseling Psychologist, 5*(1), 124-133.

Helms, J. E. (1992). Why is there no study of cultural equivalence in standardized cognitive ability testing? *American Psychologist, 47*(9), 1083-1101.

Herrnstein, R. (1971, September). I.Q. *Atlantic Monthly, 228*(3), 43-64.

Hersch, C. (1968). The discontent explosion in mental health. *American Psychologist, 23*(7), 497-506.

Highlen, P. S., & Hill, C. E. (1984). Factors affecting client change in individual counseling: Current status and theoretical speculations. In S. D. Brown & R. W. Lent (Eds.), *Handbook of counseling psychology* (pp. 334-396). New York: John Wiley.

Hills, H. I., & Strozier, A. L. (1992). Multicultural training in APA-approved counseling psychology programs: A survey. *Professional Psychology: Research and Practice, 23*(1), 43-51.

Ho, M. K. (1992). *Minority children and adolescents in therapy.* Newbury Park, CA: Sage.

Hoffman, M. A. (1993). Multiculturalism as a force in counseling clients with HIV-related concerns. *The Counseling Psychologist, 21*(4), 712-731.

Holiman, M., & Lauver, P. J. (1987). The counselor culture and client-centered practice. *Counselor Education and Supervision, 26*(3), 184-191.

Hollingshead, A. B., & Redlich, F. C. (1958). *Social class and mental illness: A community study.* New York: John Wiley.

Holsopple, J. Q., & Phelan, J. G. (1954). The skills of clinicians in analysis of projective tests. *Journal of Clinical Psychology, 10*(4), 307-320.

Ibrahim, F. A. (1991). Contribution of cultural worldview to generic counseling and development. *Journal of Counseling and Development, 70*(1), 13-19.

Ivey, A. E., Ivey, M. B., & Simek-Morgan, L. (1993). *Counseling and psychotherapy: A multicultural perspective* (3rd ed.). Boston: Allyn & Bacon.

Jackson, A. M. (1973). Psychotherapy: Factors associated with the race of the therapist. *Psychotherapy: Theory, Research and Practice, 10*(3), 273-277.

Jackson, A. M. (1976). Mental health center delivery systems and the black client. *Journal of Afro-American Issues, 4*(1), 28-34.

Jackson, A. M. (1983). Treatment issues for black patients. *Psychotherapy: Theory, Research and Practice, 20*(2), 143-151.

Jackson, A. M., Berkowitz, H., & Farley, G. K. (1974). Race as a variable affecting the treatment involvement of children. *Journal of the American Academy of Child Psychiatry, 13*(1), 20-31.

Jenkins-Hall, K., & Sacco, W. P. (1991). Effect of client race and depression on evaluations by White therapists. *Journal of Social and Cinical Psychology, 10*(3), 322-333.

Jensen, A. R. (1969). How much can we boost IQ and scholastic achievement? *Harvard Educational Review, 39*(1), 1-123.

Jones, A., & Seagull, A. A. (1977). Dimensions of the relationship between the black client and the white therapist: A theoretical overview. *American Psychologist, 32*(10), 850-855.

Jones, B. E., & Gray, B. A. (1983). Black males and psychotherapy: Theoretical issues. *American Journal of Psychotherapy, 37*(1), 77-85.

Jones, B. E., Lightfoot, O. B., Palmer, D., Wilkerson, R. G., & Williams, D. H. (1970). Problems of Black psychiatric residents in White training institutes. *American Journal of Psychiatry, 127*(6), 798-803.

Jones, D. L. (1979). African-American clients: Clinical practice issues. *Social Work, 24*(2), 112-118.

Jones, E. E. (1985). Psychotherapy and counseling with black clients. In P. Pedersen (Ed.), *Handbook of cross-cultural counseling and therapy* (pp. 173-179). Westport, CT: Greenwood Press.

Jones, E. E., & Korchin, S. J. (Eds). (1982). *Minority mental health.* New York: Praeger.

Jones, E. E., & Thorne, A. (1987). Rediscovery of the subject: Intercultural approaches to clinical assessment. *Journal of Consulting and Clinical Psychology, 55*(4), 488-495.

Jones, J. M. (1972). *Prejudice and racism.* Reading, MA: Addison-Wesley.

Jones, J. M. (1992). Understanding the mental health consequences of race: Contributions of basic social psychological processes. In D. N. Ruble, P. R. Costanzo, & M. E. Oliveri (Eds.), *The social psychology of mental health: Basic mechanisms and applications* (pp. 199-240). New York: Guilford.

Kadushin, A. (1963). Diagnosis and evaluation for (almost) all occasions. *Social Work, 8*(1), 12-19.

Kadushin, A. (1972). The racial factor in the interview. *Social Work, 17*(3), 88-98.

Kaplan, R. M., & Saccuzzo, D. P. (1993). *Psychological testing: Principles, applications, and issues* (3rd ed.). Pacific Grove, CA: Brooks/Cole.

Kardiner, A., & Ovesey, L. (1951). *The mark of oppression: Explorations in the personality of the American Negro.* Cleveland: World.

Karno, M. (1966). The enigma of ethnicity in a psychiatric clinic. *Archives of General Psychiatry, 14*(5), 516-520.

Katz, D., & Kahn, R. L. (1978). *The social psychology of organizations* (2nd ed.). New York: John Wiley.

Katz, J. H. (1985). The sociopolitical nature of counseling. *The Counseling Psychologist, 13*(4), 615-624.

Katz, P. A., & Taylor, D. A. (Eds.). (1988). *Eliminating racism: Profiles in controversy.* New York: Plenum.

Keith-Spiegel, P., & Koocher, G. P. (1985). *Ethics in psychology: Professional standards and cases.* New York: McGraw-Hill.

Kelly, T. A. (1990). The role of values in psychotherapy: A critical review of process and outcome effects. *Clinical Psychology Review, 10*(2), 171-186.

Kessler, R. C. (1979). Stress, social status and psychological distress. *Journal of Health and Social Behavior, 20*(3), 259-272.

Kleiner, R. J., Tuckman, J., & Lavell, M. (1960). Mental disorder and status based on race. *Psychiatry, 23*(3), 271-274.

Komoroff, A. L., Masuda, M., & Holmes, T. (1968). The social readjustment rating scale: A comparative study of Negro, Mexican, and white Americans. *Journal of Psychosomatic Research, 12*(2), 121-128.

Korchin, S. J. (1980). Clinical psychology and minority problems. *American Psychologist, 35*(3), 262-269.

Koriat, A., Lichtenstein, S., & Fischhoff, B. (1980). Reasons for confidence. *Journal of Experimental Psychology: Human Learning and Memory, 6*(2), 107-118.

Korman, M. (1974). National conference on levels and patterns of professional training in psychology: The major themes. *American Psychologist, 29*(6), 441-449.

Krantz, D. S., Grunberg, N. E., & Baum, A. (1985). Health psychology. *Annual Review of Psychology, 36,* 349-383.

Kuriloff, P. J. (1970). *Toward a viable public practice of psychology: A psycho-ecological model.* Unpublished doctoral dissertation, Harvard University.

LaFromboise, T., Coleman, H. L. K., & Gerton, J. (1993). Psychological impact of biculturalism: Evidence and theory. *Psychological Bulletin, 114*(3), 395-412.

Larson, P. C. (1982). Counseling special populations. *Professional Psychology, 13*(6), 843-858.

Lazarus, A. A. (1989). *The practice of multimodal therapy: Systematic, comprehensive, and effective psychotherapy.* Baltimore, MD: Johns Hopkins University Press.

Lazowick, L. M. (1955). On the nature of identification. *Journal of Abnormal and Social Psychology, 51,* 175-183.

Leigh, J. W. (1984). *Empowerment strategies for work with multi-ethnic populations.* Paper presented at the annual meeting of the Council on Social Work Education, Detroit, MI.

Leong, F. T. L., (1992). Guidelines for minimizing premature termination among Asian American clients in group counseling. *Journal for Specialists in Group Work, 17*(4), 218-228.

Lewis, J. A., Sperry, L., & Carlson, J. (1993). *Health counseling.* Pacific Grove, CA: Brooks/Cole.

Lichtenstein, S., Fischhoff, B., & Phillips, L. D. (1982). Calibration of probabilities: The state of the art to 1980. In D. Kahneman, P. Slovic, & A. Tversky (Eds.), *Judgment under uncertainty: Heuristics and biases* (pp. 306-351). Cambridge: Cambridge University Press.

Lindsey, K. P., & Paul, G. L. (1989). Involuntary commitments to public mental institutions: Issues involving the overrepresentation of Blacks and assessment of relevant functioning. *Psychological Bulletin, 106*(2), 171-183.

Locke, D. C. (1992). *Increasing multicultural understanding: A comprehensive model.* Newbury Park, CA: Sage.

Loftus, E. F., & Loftus, G. R. (1980). On the permanence of stored information in the human brain. *American Psychologist, 35*(5), 409-420.

Lopéz, S. R. (1989). Patient variable biases in clinical judgment: Conceptual overview and methodological considerations. *Psychological Bulletin, 106*(2), 184-203.

Loring, M., & Powell, B. (1988). Gender, race, and DSM-III: A study of the objectivity of psychiatric diagnostic behavior. *Journal of Health and Social Behavior, 29*(1), 1-22.

Lum, D. (1992). *Social work practice and people of color: A process-stage approach* (2nd ed.). Pacific Grove, CA: Brooks/Cole.

Mabry, M. (1988, April). Living in two worlds. *Newsweek on Campus,* p. 52.

Malgady, R. G., Rogler, L. H., & Costantino, G. (1987). Ethnocultural and linguistic bias in mental health evaluation of Hispanics. *American Psychologist, 42*(3), 228-234.

Mancucella, H. (1985). Learning theory. In Association for Advanced Training in the Behavioral Sciences (Ed.), *Preparatory course for the national/state psychology licensure examination review* (Twentieth Series) (Vol. 1, pp. 1-36). Los Angeles: Author.

Manderscheid, R., & Barrett, S. (Eds.). (1987). *Mental health, United States, 1987* (National Institute of Mental Health, DHHS Pub. No. ADM 87-1518). Washington, DC: U.S. Government Printing Office.

Marlatt, G. A. (1982). Relapse prevention: A self-control program for the treatment of addictive behaviors. In R. B. Stuart (Ed.), *Adherence, compliance and generalization in behavioral medicine* (pp. 329-378). New York: Brunner/Mazel.

Marlatt, G. A., & Gordon, J. R. (Eds.). (1985). *Relapse prevention: Maintenance strategies in the treatment of addictive behaviors.* New York: Guilford.

Martinez, C. (1988). Mexican-Americans. In L. Comas-Díaz & E. H. Griffith (Eds.), *Clinical guidelines in cross-cultural mental health* (pp. 182-203). New York: John Wiley.

Mass, J. (1967). Incidence and treatment variations between Negroes and Caucasians in mental illness. *Community Mental Health, 3*(1), 61-65.

Masserman, J. (1960). *Psychoanalysis and human values.* New York: Grune & Stratton.

Masters, J. C., & Burish, T. G. (1987). *Behavior therapy: Techniques and empirical findings* (3rd ed.). San Diego: Harcourt Brace Jovanovich.

Matarazzo, J. D. (1980). Behavioral health and behavioral medicine: Frontiers for a new health psychology. *American Psychologist, 35*(9), 807-817.

Maultsby, M. C. (1982). A historical view of blacks' distrust of psychiatry. In S. M. Turner & R. T. Jones (Eds.), *Behavior modification in black populations: Psychosocial issues and empirical findings* (pp. 39-55). New York: Plenum.

Mayo, J. A. (1974). The significance of sociocultural variables in psychiatric treatment of black outpatients. *Comprehensive Psychiatry, 15*(6), 471-482.

McCann, I. L., Sakheim, D. K., & Abrahamson, D. J. (1988). Trauma and victimization: A model of psychological adaptation. *The Counseling Psychologist, 16*(4), 531-594.

McCauley, C., Stitt, C. L., & Segal, M. (1980). Stereotyping: From prejudice to prediction. *Psychological Bulletin, 87*(1), 195-208.

McGoldrick, M., Pearce, J. K., & Giordano, J. (Eds.). (1982). *Ethnicity and family therapy.* New York: Guilford.

Meehl, P. E. (1960). The cognitive activity of the clinician. *American Psychologist, 15*(1), 19-27.

Melzack, R., & Wall, P. (1982). *The challenge of pain.* New York: Basic Books.

Mercer, K. (1984). Black communities' experience of psychiatric services. *International Journal of Social Psychiatry, 30*(1), 22-27.

Miles, R. (1989). *Racism.* London: Routledge.

Miles, R. (1993). *Racism after "race relations."* London: Routledge.

Mollica, R. (1990, March). *A look to the future.* Paper presented at the conference on mental health of immigrants and refugees, World Federation for Mental Health and Hogg Foundation for Mental Health, Houston, TX.

Montagu, A. (Ed.). (1964). *The concept of race.* New York: Free Press.

Morrow, K. A., & Deidan, C. T. (1992). Bias in the counseling process: How to recognize and avoid it. *Journal of Counseling and Development, 70*(5), 571-577.

Moses-Zirkes, S. (1993, August). APA asks Congress to fund more training for minorities. *APA Monitor,* p. 57.

Moy, S. (1992). A culturally sensitive, psychoeducational model for understanding and treating Asian-American clients. *Journal of Psychology and Christianity, 11*(4), 358-367.

Mueller, D. P., Edwards, D. W., & Yarvis, R. M. (1977). Stressful life events and psychiatric symptomatology: Change or undesirability? *Journal of Health and Social Behavior, 18*(3), 307-317.

Mukherjee, S., Shukla, S., Woodle, J., Rosen, A. M., & Olarte, S. (1983). Misdiagnosis of schizophrenia in bipolar patients: A multiethnic comparison. *American Journal of Psychiatry, 140*(12), 1571-1574.

Nietzel, M. T., Bernstein, D. A., & Milich, R. (1994). *Introduction to clinical psychology* (4th ed.). Englewood Cliffs, NJ: Prentice Hall.

Okun, B. F. (1992). *Effective helping: Interviewing and counseling techniques* (4th ed.). Pacific Grove, CA: Brooks/Cole.

Pavkov, T. W., Lewis, D. A., Lyons, J. S. (1989). Psychiatric diagnoses and racial bias: An empirical investigation. *Professional Psychology: Research and Practice, 20*(6), 364-368.

Pedersen, P. (1987). Ten frequent assumptions of cultural bias in counseling. *Journal of Multicultural Counseling and Development, 15*(1), 16-24.

Pedersen, P. (1994). *A handbook for developing multicultural awareness* (2nd ed.). Alexandria, VA: American Counseling Association.

Pedersen, P. B. (1990, August). Interracial collaboration among counseling psychologists. In J. G. Ponterotto (Chair), *The White American researcher in multicultural counseling: Significance and challenges.* Symposium presented at the 98th Annual Convention of the American Psychological Association, Boston, MA.

Peoples, V. Y., & Dell, D. M. (1975). Black and white student preferences for counselor roles. *Journal of Counseling Psychology, 22*(6) 529-534.

Phares, E. J. (1992). *Clinical psychology: Concepts, methods, and profession* (4th ed.). Pacific Grove, CA: Brooks/Cole.

Phinney, J. S., Lochner, B. T., & Murphy, R. (1990). Ethnic identity development and psychological adjustment in adolescence. In A. R. Stiffman & L. E. Davis (Eds.), *Ethnic issues in adolescent mental health* (pp. 53-72). Newbury Park, CA: Sage.

Pietrofesa, J. J., Hoffman, A., & Splete, H. H. (1984). *Counseling: An introduction* (2nd ed.). Boston: Houghton Mifflin.

Pinderhughes, C. A. (1973). Racism and psychotherapy. In C. V. Willie, B. M. Kramer, & B. S. Brown (Eds.), *Racism and mental health: Essays* (pp. 61-121). Pittsburgh: University of Pittsburgh Press.

Pinderhughes, E. (1989). *Understanding race, ethnicity, and power: The key to efficacy in clinical practice.* New York: Free Press.

Ponce, F. Q., & Atkinson, D. R. (1989). Mexican-American acculturation, counselor ethnicity, counseling style, and perceived counselor credibility. *Journal of Counseling Psychology, 36*(2), 203-208.

Ponterotto, J. G. (1987). Counseling Mexican Americans: A multimodal approach. *Journal of Counseling and Development, 65*(6), 308-312.

Ponterotto, J. G., & Casas, J. M. (1987). In search of multicultural competence within counselor education programs. *Journal of Counseling and Development, 65*(8), 430-434.

Ponterotto, J. G., & Pedersen, P. B. (1993). *Preventing prejudice: A guide for counselors and educators.* Newbury Park, CA: Sage.

President's Commission on Mental Health. (1978). *Task panel report to the President* (Vols. 1-4). Washington, DC: U.S. Government Printing Office.

Ramirez, M. (1983). *Psychology of the Americas: Mestizo perspectives on personality and mental health.* New York: Pergamon Press.

Ramos-McKay, J. M., Comas-Díaz, L., & Rivera, L. A. (1988). Puerto Ricans. In L. Comas-Díaz & E. E. H. Griffith (Eds.), *Clinical guidelines in cross-cultural mental health* (pp. 204-232). New York: John Wiley.

Reed, R. (1988). Education and achievement of young black males. In J. T. Gibbs (Ed.), *Young, black and male in America: An endangered species* (pp. 37-96). Dover, MA: Auburn House.

Reiff, R. (1967). Mental health manpower and institutional change. In E. L. Cowen, E. A. Gardner, & M. Zax (Eds.), *Emergent approaches to mental health problems* (pp. 74-88). New York: Appleton-Century-Crofts.

Reiss, S., & Szyszko, J. (1983). Diagnostic overshadowing and professional experience with mentally retarded persons. *American Journal of Mental Deficiency, 87*(4), 396-402.

Rendon, M. (1984). Myths and stereotypes in minority groups. *International Journal of Social Psychiatry, 30*(4), 297-309.

Reynolds, C. R., & Brown, R. T. (1984). Bias in mental testing: An introduction to the issues. In C. R. Reynolds & R. T. Brown (Eds.), *Perspectives on bias in mental testing* (pp. 1-39). New York: Plenum.

Reynolds, G. S. (1968). *A primer of operant conditioning.* Glenview, IL: Scott, Foresman.

Ridley, C. R. (1978). Cross-cultural counseling: A multivariate analysis. *Viewpoints in teaching and learning, 54*(1), 43-50.

Ridley, C. R. (1984). Clinical treatment of the nondisclosing black client: A therapeutic paradox. *American Psychologist, 39*(11), 1234-1244.

Ridley, C. R. (1985a). Imperatives for ethnic and cultural relevance in psychology training programs. *Professional Psychology: Research and Practice, 16*(5), 611-622.

Ridley, C. R. (1985b). Pseudo-transference in interracial psychotherapy: An operant paradigm. *Journal of Contemporary Psychotherapy, 15*(1), 29-36.

Ridley, C. R. (1986a). Cross-cultural counseling in theological context. *Journal of Psychology and Theology, 14*(4), 288-297.

Ridley, C. R. (1986b). Diagnosis as a function of race pairing and client self-disclosure. *Journal of Cross-Cultural Psychology, 17*(3), 337-351.

Ridley, C. R. (1986c). Optimum service delivery to the black client. *American Psychologist, 41*(2), 226-227.

Ridley, C. R. (1989). Racism in counseling as an adversive behavioral process. In P. B. Pedersen, J. G. Draguns, W. J. Lonner, & J. E. Trimble (Eds.), *Counseling across cultures* (3rd ed.) (pp. 55-77). Honolulu: University of Hawaii Press.

Ridley, C. R., Mendoza, D., & Kanitz, B. (1994). Multicultural training: Reexamination, operationalization, and integration. *The Counseling Psychologist, 22*(2), 227-289

Ridley, C. R., & Mendoza, D. W. (1993). Putting organizational effectiveness into practice: The preeminent consultation task. *Journal of Counseling and Development, 72*(2), 168-177.

Ridley, C. R., Mendoza, D. W., Kanitz, B. E., Angermeier, L., & Zenk, R. (1994). Cultural sensitivity in multicultural counseling: A perceptual schema model. *Journal of Counseling Psychology, 41*(2), 125-136.

Ridley, C. R., & Tan, S-Y. (1986). Unintentional paradoxes and potential pitfalls in paradoxical psychotherapy. *The Counseling Psychologist, 14*(2), 303-308.

Riessman, F., & Miller, S. M. (1964). Social change versus the psychiatric world view. *American Journal of Orthopsychiatry, 34*(1), 29-38.

Rivers, L. W., Henderson, D. M., Jones, R. L., Ladner, J. A., & Williams, R. L. (1975). Mosaic of labels for black children. In N. Hobbs (Ed.), *Issues in the classification of children* (Vol. 2, pp. 213-245). San Francisco: Jossey-Bass.

Robinson, T. (1993). The intersections of gender, class, race, and culture: On seeing clients whole. *Journal of Multicultural Counseling and Development, 21*(1), 50-58.

Rogers, C. R. (1961). *On becoming a person: A therapist's view of psychotherapy.* Boston: Houghton Mifflin.

Rogler, L. H. (1993). Culture in psychiatric diagnosis: An issue of scientific accuracy. *Psychiatry, 56*(4), 324-327.

Rosado, J. W., Jr., & Elias, M. J. (1993). Ecological and psychocultural mediators in the delivery of services for urban, culturally diverse Hispanic clients. *Professional Psychology: Research and Practice, 24*(4), 450-459.

Rosen, H., & Frank, J. D. (1962). Negroes in psychotherapy. *American Journal of Psychiatry, 119*(5), 456-460.

Rosenhan, D. L. (1973). On being sane in insane places. *Science, 179*(4070), 250-258.

Ross, L. (1977). The intuitive psychologist and his shortcomings: Distortions in the attribution process. In L. Berkowitz (Ed.), *Advances in experimental social psychology* (Vol. 10, pp. 173-220). New York: Academic Press.

Rousseve, R. (1987, March/April). A black American youth torn between cultures. *The Humanist,* pp. 5-8.

Ruch, F. L. (1967). *Psychology and life* (7th ed.). Glenview, IL: Scott, Foresman.

Rushton, J. P. (1988). Race differences in behaviour: A review and evolutionary analysis. *Journal of Personality and Individual Differences, 9,* 1009-1024.

Ryan, W. (1971). *Blaming the victim.* New York: Vintage Books.

Sabshin, M., Diesenhaus, H., & Wilkerson, R. (1970). Dimensions of institutional racism in psychiatry. *American Journal of Psychiatry, 127*(6), 787-793.

Sager, C. J., Brayboy, T. L., & Waxenberg, B. R. (1972). Black patient-white therapist. *American Journal of Orthopsychiatry, 42*(3), 415-423.

Samuda, R. J. (1975). *Psychological testing of American minorities: Issues and consequences.* New York: Dodd, Mead.

Sandler, J., & Freud, A. (1985). *The analysis of defense: The ego and the mechanisms of defense revisited.* New York: International Universities Press.

Schaefer, R. T. (1988). *Racial and ethnic groups* (3rd ed.). Glenview, IL: Scott, Foresman.

Schofield, W. (1964). *Psychotherapy: The purchase of friendship.* Englewood Cliffs, NJ: Prentice Hall.

Schonbachler, P., & Spengler, P. M. (1992). Borderline personality disorder and signs of sexual abuse: Do psychologists test a sexual trauma hypothesis? Unpublished manuscript.

Scissons, E. H. (1993). *Counseling for results: Principles and practices of helping.* Pacific Grove, CA: Brooks/Cole.

Sedlacek, W. E., & Brooks, G. C. (1976). *Racism in American education: A model for change.* Chicago: Nelson-Hall.

Shervington, W. W. (1976). Racism, professionalism, elitism: Their effect on the mental health delivery system. *Journal of the National Medical Association, 68*(2), 91-96.

Shockley, W. (1971). Negro IQ deficit: Failure of a "malicious coincidence" model warrants new research proposals. *Review of Educational Research, 41*(3), 227-248.

Shuey, A. M. (1966). *The testing of Negro intelligence.* New York: Social Science Press.

Skinner, B. F. (1957). *Verbal behavior.* New York: Appleton-Century-Crofts.

Smedes, L. B. (1984). *Forgive and forget: Healing the hurts we don't deserve.* San Francisco: Harper & Row.

Smirnow, B. W., & Bruhn, A. R. (1984). Encopresis in a Hispanic boy: Distinguishing pathology from cultural differences. *Psychotherapy: Theory, Research and Practice, 21*(1), 24-30.

Snowden, L. R., & Cheung, F. K. (1990). Use of inpatient mental health services by members of ethnic minority groups. *American Psychologist, 45*(3), 347-355.

Snyder, M. (1982, July). Self-fulfilling stereotypes. *Psychology Today,* pp. 60, 65, 67-68.

Snyder, M., & Uranowitz, S. W. (1978). Reconstructing the past: Some cognitive consequences of person perception. *Journal of Personality and Social Psychology, 36*(9), 941-950.

Solomon, A. (1992). Clinical diagnosis among diverse populations: A multicultural perspective. *Families in Society: The Journal of Contemporary Human Services, 73*(6), 371-377.

Solomon, P. (1988). Racial factors in mental health service utilization. *Psychosocial Rehabilitiation Journal, 11*(3), 3-12.

Spengler, P. M. (1992, August). Application of scientist-professional assessment to practice and graduate curriculum. In P. M. Spengler (Chair), *Scientist-professional model of psychological assessment.* Symposium conducted at the annual meeting of the American Psychological Association, Washington, DC.

Spengler, P. M., Blustein, D. L., & Strohmer, D. C. (1990). Diagnostic and treatment overshadowing of vocational problems by personal problems. *Journal of Counseling Psychology, 37*(4) 372-381.

Spengler, P., Strohmer, D. C., Dorau, L., and Gard, T. (1994, August). Psychological masquerade: Comparison of counseling and clinical psychologists, psychiatrists, and physicians. Paper presented at the annual meeting of the American Psychological Association, Los Angeles, CA.

Sperry, L. (1988). Biopsychosocial therapy: An integrative approach for tailoring treatment. *Individual Psychology, 44*(2), 225-235.

Spurlock, J. (1985). Assessment and therapeutic intervention of black children. *Journal of American Academy of Child Psychiatry, 24*(2) 168-174.

Stack, L. C., Lannon, P. B., & Miley, A. D. (1983). Accuracy of clinicians' expectancies for psychiatric rehospitalization. *American Journal of Community Psychology, 11*(1), 99-113.

Stanton, W. R. (1960). *The leopard's spots: Scientific attitudes toward race in America, 1815-1859.* Chicago: University of Chicago Press.

Steele, S. (1990). *The content of our character: A new vision of race in America.* New York: Harper Perennial.

Steinberg, M. D., Pardes, H., Bjork, D., & Sporty, L. (1977). Demographic and clinical characteristics of black psychiatric patients in a private general hospital. *Hospital and Community Psychiatry, 28*(2), 128-132.

Stevenson, H. C., & Renard, G. (1993). Trusting ole' wise owls: Therapeutic use of cultural strengths in African-American families. *Professional Psychology: Research and Practice, 24*(4), 433-442.

Strohmer, D. C., & Shivy, V. A. (1992, August). Judgmental and inferential errors in counseling. In P. M. Spengler (Chair), *Scientist-professional model of psychological assessment.* Symposium conducted at the annual meeting of the American Psychological Association, Washington, DC.

Strong, S. R. (1964). Verbal conditioning and counseling research. *Personnel and Guidance Journal, 42*(7), 660-669.

Sue, D. W. (1977). Counseling the culturally different: A conceptual analysis. *Personnel and Guidance Journal, 55*(7), 422-425.

Sue, D. W. (1978). Eliminating cultural oppression in counseling: Toward a general theory. *Journal of Counseling Psychology, 25*(5), 419-428.

Sue, D. W., & Sue, D. (1977). Barriers to effective cross-cultural counseling. *Journal of Counseling Psychology, 24*(5), 420-429.

Sue, D. W., & Sue, D. (1990). *Counseling the culturally different: Theory and practice* (2nd ed.). New York: John Wiley.

Sue, D. W., & Sue, S. (1972). Counseling Chinese-Americans. *Personnel and Guidance Journal, 50*(8), 637-644.

Sue, S. (1977). Community mental health services to minroity groups: Some optimism, some pessimism. *American Psychologist, 32*(8), 616-624.

Sue, S., & Zane, N. (1987). The role of culture and cultural techniques in psychotherapy: A critique and reformulation. *American Psychologist, 42*(1), 37-45.

Sutton, R. G., & Kessler, M. (1986). National study of the effects of clients' socioeconomic status on clinical psychologists' professional judgments. *Journal of Consulting and Clinical Psychology, 54*(2), 275-276.

Sykes, D. K. (1987). An approach to working with black youth in cross-cultural therapy. *Clinical Social Work Journal, 15*(3), 260-270.

Szapocznik, J., & Kurtines, W. (1980). Acculturation, biculturalism, and adjustment among Cuban Americans. In A. Padilla (Ed.), *Acculturation: Theory, models, and some new findings* (pp. 27-42). Boulder, CO: Westview.

Szapocznik, J., & Kurtines, W. M. (1993). Family psychology and cultural diversity: Opportunities for theory, research, and application. *American Psychologist, 48*(4), 400-407.

Szapocznik, J., Scopetta, M. A., Arnalde, M. & Kurtines, W. (1978). Cuban value structure: Treatment implications. *Journal of Consulting and Clinical Psychology, 46*(5), 961-970.

Tajfel, H. (Ed.). (1978). *Differentiation between social groups: Studies in the social psychology of intergroup relations.* London: Academic Press.

Taylor, S. E. (1990). Health psychology: The science and the field. *American Psychologist, 45*(1), 40-50.

Teichner, V., Cadden, J. J., & Berry, G. W. (1981). The Puerto Rican patient: Some historical, cultural and psychological aspects. *Journal of the American Academy of Psychoanalysis, 9*(2), 277-289.

Terman, L. M. (1916). *The measurement of intelligence: An explanation of and a complete guide for the use of the Stanford revision and extension of the Binet-Simon intelligence scale.* Boston: Houghton Mifflin.

Teyber, E. (1992). *Interpersonal process in psychotherapy: A guide for clinical practice* (2nd ed.). Pacific Grove, CA: Brooks/Cole.

Tharp, R. G. (1991). Cultural diversity and treatment of children. *Journal of Consulting and Clinical Psychology, 59*(6), 799-812.

Thomas, A. (1962). Pseudo-transference reactions due to cultural stereotyping. *American Journal of Orthopsychiatry, 32*(5), 894-900.

Thomas, A., & Sillen, S. (1972). *Racism and psychiatry.* Secaucus, NJ: Citadel.

Thomason, T. C. (1991). Counseling Native Americans: An introduction for non-Native American counselors. *Journal of Counseling and Development, 69*(4), 321-327.

Thompson, C. E., Worthington, R., & Atkinson, D. R. (1994). Counselor content orientation, counselor race, and Black women's cultural mistrust and self-disclosures. *Journal of Counseling Psychology, 41*(2), 155-161.

Thompson, J. W., Blueye, H. B., Smith, C. R., & Walker, R. D. (1983). Cross-cultural curriculum content in psychiatric residency training: An American Indian and Alaska Native perspective. In J. C. Chunn II, P. J. Dunston, & F. Ross-Sherrif (Eds.), *Mental health and people of color: Curriculum development and change* (pp. 269-288). Washington, DC: Howard University Press.

Thouless, R. H. (1974). *Straight and crooked thinking: Thirty-eight dishonest tricks of debate.* London: Pan Books.

Tomes, H. (1994, June). Minority recruitment, retention is a priority. *APA Monitor,* p. 35.

Triandis, H. C., Malpass, R. S., & Davidson, A. R. (1973). Psychology and culture. *Annual Review of Psychology, 24,* 355-378.

Turner, R. J., & Cumming, J. (1967). Theoretical malaise and community mental health. In E. L. Cowen, E. A. Gardner, & M. Zax (Eds.), *Emergent approaches to mental health problems* (pp. 40-62). New York: Appleton-Century-Crofts.

Uba, L. (1982). Meeting the mental health needs of Asian Americans: Mainstream or segregated services. *Professional Psychology, 13*(2), 215-221.

U. S. Department of Health and Human Services. (1986). *Report of the secretary's task force on black and minority health: Vol. 5.* Washington, DC: Author.

Usher, C. H. (1989). Recognizing cultural bias in counseling theory and practice: The case of Rogers. *Journal of Multicultural Counseling and Development, 17*(2), 62-71.

vanden Berghe, P. (1967). *Race and racism: A comparative perspective.* New York: John Wiley.

Vargas, L. A., & Koss-Chioino, J. D. (Eds.). (1992). *Working with culture: Psychotherapeutic interventions with ethnic minority children and adolescents.* San Francisco: Jossey-Bass.

Vontress, C. E. (1981). Racial and ethnic barriers in counseling. In P. B. Pedersen, J. G. Draguns, W. J. Lonner, & J. E. Trimble (Eds.), *Counseling across cultures* (2nd ed.) (pp. 87-107). Honolulu: University Press of Hawaii.

Wade, J. C. (1993). Institutional racism: An analysis of the mental health system. *American Journal of Orthopsychiatry, 63*(4), 536-544.

Wallace, A. F. C. (1970). *Culture and personality* (2nd ed.). New York: Random House.

Warren, R. C., Jackson, A. M., Nugaris, J., & Farley, G. K. (1973). Differential attitudes of black and white patients toward treatment in a child guidance clinic. *American Journal of Orthopsychiatry, 43*(3), 384-393.

Watkins, B., Cowan, M., & Davis. W. (1975). Differential diagnosis imbalance as a race-related phenomenon. *Journal of Clinical Psychology, 31,* 267-268.

Watson, D. L., & Tharp, R. G. (1993). *Self-directed behavior: Self-modification for personal adjustment* (6th ed.). Pacific Grove, CA: Brooks/Cole.

Watzlawick, P., Beavin, J. H., & Jackson, D. D. (1967). *Pragmatics of human communication: A study of interactional patterns, pathologies, and paradoxes.* New York: Norton.

Wells, G. L. (1982). Attribution and reconstructive memory. *Journal of Experimental Social Psychology, 18*(5), 447-463.

Westermeyer, J. (1987). Cultural factors in clinical assessment. *Journal of Consulting and Clinical Psychology, 55*(4), 471-478.

Wierzbicki, M., & Pekarik, G. (1993). A meta-analysis of psychotherapy dropout. *Professional Psychology: Research and Practice, 24*(2), 190-195.

Willie, C. V., Kramer, B. M., & Brown, B. S. (Eds.). (1973). *Racism and mental health: Essays.* Pittsburgh: University of Pittsburgh Press.

Wills, T. A. (1978). Perceptions of clients by professional helpers. *Psychological Bulletin, 85*(5), 968-1000.

Wintrob, R. M., & Harvey, Y. K. (1981). The self-awareness factor in intercultural psychotherapy: Some personal reflections. In P. B. Pedersen, J. G. Draguns, W. J. Lonner, & J. E. Trimble (Eds.), *Counseling across cultures* (2nd ed.) (pp. 108-132). Honolulu: University Press of Hawaii.

Word, C. O., Zanna, M. P., & Cooper, J. (1974). The nonverbal mediation of self-fulfilling prophecies in interracial interaction. *Journal of Experimental Social Psychology, 10*(2), 109-120.

Wrenn, C. G. (1962). The culturally encapsulated counselor. *Harvard Educational Review, 32*(4), 444-449.

Wrenn, C. G. (1985). Afterward: The culturally encapsulated counselor revisited. In P. Pedersen (Ed.), *Handbook of cross-cultural counseling and therapy* (pp. 323-329). Westport, CT: Greenwood Press.

Wyatt, G. E. (1977). A comparison of the scaling of Afro-American life-change events. *Journal of Human Stress, 3*(1), 13-18.

Yamamoto, J., James, Q. C., Bloombaum, M., & Hattem, J. (1967). Racial factors in patient selection. *American Journal of Psychiatry, 124*(5), 84-90.

Yamamoto, J., James, Q. C., & Palley, N. (1968). Cultural problems in psychiatric therapy. *Archives of General Psychiatry, 19*(1), 45-49.

Yee, A. H., Fairchild, H. H., Weizmann, F., & Wyatt, G. E. (1993). Addressing psychology's problems with race. *American Psychologist, 48*(11), 1132-1140.

Young, M. E. (1992). *Counseling methods and techniques: An eclectic approach.* New York: Macmillan.

Zuckerman, M. (1990). Some dubious premises in research and theory on racial differences: Scientific, social, and ethical issues. *American Psychologist, 45*(12), 1297-1303.

Index

About the Author

Charles R. Ridley is Associate Professor and Director of Training of the Counseling Psychology Program at Indiana University, Bloomington. Prior to his arrival at Indiana in 1990, he held academic appointments at the University of Maryland and the Graduate School of Psychology at Fuller Theological Seminary. He also was a consulting psychologist with Personnel Decisions, Inc. He holds a Ph.D. in Counseling Psychology from the University of Minnesota.

Dr. Ridley has published numerous journal articles and book chapters. In addition to his interest in multicultural counseling and training, he has written on organizational consultation and on the use of religious resources in psychotherapy. He has served on the editorial boards of *The Counseling Psychologist* and *Journal of Psychology and Theology.* From 1992 to 1993, he was a fellow in the Academic Leadership Program of the Committee on Institutional Cooperation.